SYKESVILLE
Past and Present

by

Healan Barrow

Edited by

Samuel J. Baum and Linda Greenberg

A Greenberg Publication

Copyright 1987

Greenberg Publishing Company, Inc.
7566 Main Street
Sykesville, MD 21784
(301) 795-7447

Manufactured in the United States of America

Greenberg Publishing Company, Inc. offers the world's largest
selection of Lionel, American Flyer and other toy train
publications as well as a selection of books on other collectibles
such as space toys, marbles, and dollhouses. Our catalogue is
available for $2.00 refundable with your order.

Greenberg Shows, Inc. sponsors the world's largest public
model railroad shows. The shows feature extravagant
operating model railroads for N, HO, O, Standard and 1 Gauges
as well as huge marketplace for buying and selling nearly all
model railroad equipment. The shows also feature, a large
selection of dollhouses and dollhouse furnishings. Shows are
currently offered in metropolitan Boston, Long Island in New
York, Philadelphia, Pittsburgh, Baltimore, Norfolk, New
Jersey and Florida. To receive the current show listing, please
send a self-addressed stamped envelope marked "Train Show
Schedule" to the address above.

Library of Congress Cataloging-in-Publication Data

Barrow, Healan.
    Sykesville, Past and Present.

    Bibliography: p.
    Includes index.
    1. Sykesville (Md.) — Description — Tours.
2. Sykesville (Md.) — History. 3. Historic buildings —
Maryland — Sykesville — Guide-books. I. Greenberg, Linda.
II. Baum, Samuel J. III. Title.
F189.S95B37 1987   975.2'77   87-19766
ISBN 0-89778-018-3

Table of Contents

Maps

Acknowledgements

Many Sykesville residents contributed their time and memories to this book:

Celius L. Brown spent countless hours reliving memories that made my hand-drawn map of Sykesville's businesses and homes come alive. **Dorothy Schafer's** stories and ideas often pointed me in the right direction for research. And **W. Almer Forthman's** anecdotes and generous patience helped answer many questions.

Discovering Sykesville's history was made a lot easier with the help of **William Frederick Church**, who spent 42 years with the Sykesville Herald, first as an employee in the print shop and later as editor, president, and owner of the newspaper. Ask him about any event in Sykesville, and he can pull out a bound copy of the newspaper and show you the facts. Mr. Church also provided some of the historical photographs which appear in this book.

William B. Welling, Jr.'s many memories of Sykesville also gave me a flavor for town life in the 1930's. He typed numerous pages of notes to guide me in my search.

Mrs. Lillian Berry Brown remembered stories from her grandparents who survived the flood of 1868 and helped in rebuilding the town on the Carroll County side of the Patapsco.

Mrs. Thelma Wimmer graciously read an early version of this manuscript and made many helpful comments. As chairperson of the **Sykesville Historic Preservation Commission** the information she has amassed has provided valuable insight to the town's past.

James Schumacher, the Town Manager, whose vision of the future provides the energy that sets Sykesville's "new beginnings" in motion.

Other Sykesville residents also gave me information and in many cases tours of their homes. They included **Mr. and Mrs. Richard Bagley, Poly Ely, Roland Ferguson, Harold Gaither, Jack Harris, Becky and Jon Herman, Jeannette and Mike Kasnia, Esther and Harold Mercer, Craig and Charlie Taylor, Jay and Rob Treganza, Jerry Trescott, Howard Warfield, Anita Wilson, Eleanor Wood, Mr. and Mrs. Edward Zable**, and many others who stopped to talk and give me encouragement.

Outside of Sykesville, there were others who, in one way or another, assisted in the making of this book:

Peter Kurtze of the Maryland Historical Trust whose valuable comments helped to clarify certain issues particularly in weeding out the fiction from the facts. **Herbert H. Harwood, Jr.** whose information regarding the B & O Railroad helped to clear up some of the "foggy" history of this early railroad town. And **Maxine Warfield** who read an early version of this manuscript and whose comments were most helpful.

Thank you to all who are mentioned above, and to those whose names have been inadvertently left out, your help was no less appreciated.

At the **Greenberg Publishing Company, Maureen Crum's** paste-up work and renderings of the maps helped to make this an easy book to use. **Bruce Greenberg** shot many of the photographs, as did **Maury Feinstein** who also printed the negatives. A very special thank you goes to **Samuel Baum** for his excellent suggestions and editing, and to **Linda Greenberg** who knew that Sykesville's past and present would make a good book.

Healan Barrow

July 1987

Dedication

To Thelma C. Wimmer, the unofficial historian for the Town of Sykesville:

— for the countless hours she has spent unlocking the historical secrets of the town;
— for encouraging others to keep the history alive;
— and for providing the impetus for Sykesville's rejuvination.

Introduction

SYKESVILLE — Hidden Treasures from the Past

When Linda Greenberg asked me to write the history of Sykesville, I didn't know what reaction I would get from the townspeople. After all, I am an outsider who lives in the next county.

To say I was welcomed is an understatement. People spent hours sharing memories and explaining why events happened. A number of times the person I was interviewing would actually take me to the place we were talking about. I have been allowed to climb attic stairs, poke through basements and see family papers.

At times I felt like I was putting together a jigsaw puzzle of facts and memories. The picture of Sykesville kept growing larger and more colorful. The more I learned, the more I wanted to learn.

Sykesville is a treasure-trove of anecdotes and stories — so many that all of them cannot be recorded. I cannot even say I have picked out the best ones because all were interesting. But I did try to concentrate on the history of the town. And I did discover that Sykesville is indeed a place of many hidden treasures.

Map I — Sykesville's Location in Carroll County

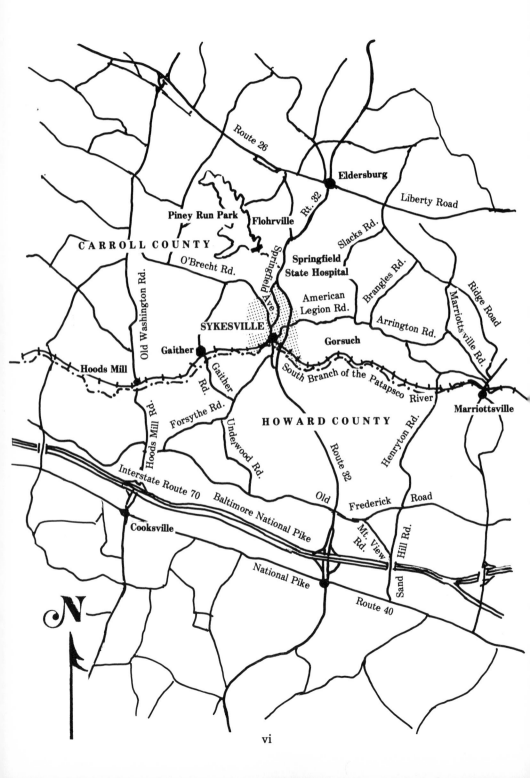

Tales of Sykesville — Folklore and History

A first glimpse of Sykesville from Route 32 suggests a bare notion of a town — a cluster of timeworn buildings in a valley below the highway. The town nestles at the edge of the south branch of the Patapsco River. On a map, Sykesville is also at the edge of the southeastern Carroll County border.

The river forms the southern boundary line of both the town and the county, however, some of the farms and homes in neighboring Howard County have shared in Sykesville history. In fact, Sykesville's zip code 21784 takes in a tiny fraction of its southern neighbor.

The main entrance road into the town is off of Rt. 32, just 3 miles from its intersection with U.S. Rt. 70.

This view of Sykesville's Main Street was snapped in about 1906. It was photographed from approximately the bottom of the hill on which the Town House stands today. Courtesy of the Sykesville Historic Preservation Commission.

The Beginnings

Flourishing grain fields, rich spring-fed soil and the bubbling southern branch of the Patapsco river probably attracted James Sykes to what is now Sykesville. In 1825, he bought 1,000 acres of land, in different tracts, which included the future town.

The son of a prominent Baltimore merchant, Sykes recognized the potential for a flour mill. And seemly nature had already laid out the best location for it.

The land on the north side of the river (now the present town in Carroll County) had steep hills dotted with many springs. It was a beautiful setting but certainly not a place to build. On the south side of the Patapsco in Howard County, however, the land was flat. Plus there was already an old saw- and grist-mill located there. Sykes rebuilt this mill by 1831 and probably had a steady stream of customers from the near-by farms. He later also built a cotton factory (see The Howard County Cotton Factory, pg. 5).

However, it was another wealthy Baltimore merchant who set the stage for Sykes to develop his new land purchase into a thriving business. William Patterson, a Scotch-Irish merchant and shipbuilder, was known as one of the richest men in Maryland at that time. He had his summer home near Sykesville at Springfield, a portion of which is now Springfield Hospital Center. In the early 1800s, Springfield was a 3,000 acre estate with some of the best farmland in the area.

Patterson was also one of the original directors of the Baltimore & Ohio (B & O) Railroad, and it is said that when the railroad needed construction money, Patterson gave assistance. However, he stipulated that the line should go near his summer estate at Springfield.

Sykes quickly took advantage of the railroad that would now come through his property, and, in 1831, he built a four-story stone hotel and tavern to provide a rest stop for passengers. At the time, the train cars were pulled by slow moving horses,

Sykes' Hotel and Tavern may also have served as the town's original train station. Photograph courtesy of the Maryland Historical Society in Baltimore.

and Sykesville was considered the midpoint between Baltimore and Frederick. When the steam engine replaced the horse, a stop at Sykes Hotel was not as critical. The hotel then became known as a summer resort which attracted railroad officials as well as other Baltimoreans.

The four-story hotel was 50 feet by 74 feet and had 47 rooms. It was located on the flat land on the Howard County side of the river. The stone building appears to have been a simple, compact, L-shaped structure with a hip-roof and wide two-story porches and railings on each side of the L. The hotel was destroyed in the flood of 1868.

The B & O Railroad
The First Public Rail Service in the U.S.

Sykesville probably owes most of its original vitality and prosperity to the railroad. Before the line was put in, the main east-west route was the old National Pike, located some distance from the town. The railroad was the first long-distance rail enterprise in the country, and Sykesville's early commerce revolved around it.

When the railroad was conceived in 1828, the engineers decided to locate the route between Baltimore and Frederick beside the curving Patapsco River, taking advantage of the relatively flat land. The railroad through Sykesville was to be B & O's original main line, finally linking Baltimore with the Ohio River, first to Wheeling and later to Cincinnati.

At the time, railroad transportation was in its infancy and there was very little past experience that the designers and construction engineers could call upon in developing the system. The railroad men didn't know what kind of base to lay their rails across and so laid them on long granite stringers. It did not take much time before the engineers realized that the rigid, unyielding granite created an uncomfortable ride, and they replaced them with the familiar wooden ties that we see today.

However, remnants of the stringers can still be found in Sykesville. One of the granite strips was used in the construction of St. Barnabas Church, and another was moved to the cemetery behind the Church (no. 68 on Tour 2). And, if you look carefully for the rail indentations, you can see that sections of a stringer were also used for the stone gate posts on Springfield Avenue (no. 59 on Tour 2).

Sykesville also has the distinction of receiving the first American troops ever transported by train. In June of 1831, over one hundred construction workers went on strike because they had not been paid by the contractor. He had taken the money due the workmen and fled. Railroad officials could not reason with the angry men who threatened violence, and the Baltimore militia was called out. They came to Sykesville by train and arrested the ringleaders.

The line remained as Baltimore's sole route to the west until 1873, when the railway out of Washington was completed. After that, west heading passenger trains were routed via Washington D.C., and the Sykesville route became known as the "Old Main Line."

Local service, which started in late 1831, continued on the "Old Main" serving Sykesville, Frederick and other communities along the line. Sykesville's station was the hub for freight and passenger service. Students rode the train to either Mt. Airy or Ellicott City to go to high school. Farmers and local businesses depended on the train to ship or receive their produce and products.

Shortly after the turn of the century, the line was substantially rebuilt to handle heavy tonnage freight trains — particularly coal trains. In 1949, passenger service was suspended on the "Old Main Line" and the Sykesville Station was closed.

Locomotives like this one may have been some of the first to travel the B & O rails. Photograph courtesy of Herbert H. Harwood, Jr.

That stretch of railway came close to abandonment after it was damaged by Hurricane Agnes in June 1972. It was eventually rebuilt and, for the moment, continues as a major freight route — although active freight business along the line has virtually disappeared.

William Patterson's Springfield and the Bonaparte Romance

The summer mansion of William Patterson (which burned in 1912) started as a log house in the early 1800s. Through the years a number of additions were made and, eventually, the logs of the original six rooms were covered with wainscoting.

According to some sources, Patterson tried to keep his daughter Elizabeth, or more commonly known as Betsy (b. 1785, d. 1879), at Springfield in the hopes that she would get over her infatuation with Prince Jerome Bonaparte, brother of Napoleon. Betsy had met the Prince in Baltimore at the races and there was an instant mutual attraction. But, Patterson had little love for royalty and was eager to avoid any complications.

Elizabeth Patterson as she must have appeared to Prince Jerome Bonaparte. This is a pastel by D'Almaine after Gilbert Stuart's portrait. Courtesy of the Maryland Historical Society in Baltimore.

The story goes that Betsy was at Springfield when she heard that a ball was to be given for Prince Jerome in Baltimore. Supposedly, her father locked up all the horses and her dresses so that she couldn't go.

Betsy climbed down a rain spout and rode a mule the 20 miles over Liberty Road to Baltimore. Her maid, riding another mule, carried her ball dress. She arrived when the ball was at its height and the prince fell desperately in love with her.

Some historical sources say that William Patterson may not have been living at Springfield at the time of the romance, and, consequently, Betsy's daring ride may be more romantic fiction than fact. But it is true that Betsy, against her father's wishes, did attend the ball and later married the Prince on Christmas Eve, 1803.

Napoleon was also against the match. When Jerome took his new wife to Europe, French troops surrounded their ship as it landed at Lisbon. Betsy was not allowed to disembark, and she and Jerome were never together again.

Betsy went on to England where their son, Jerome Napoleon Bonaparte, was born in 1805. Eventually, Napoleon insisted that his brother marry a European princess even though the Pope would not sanction a divorce.

In the 1820s, Betsy had a brilliant social career in European society. And later, one of her grandsons became a colonel in the French Army. For the last forty-five years of her life, she chose to stay in a boarding house in Baltimore. Although her father left her very little money, she was a shrewd business woman and at her death left a large estate to her grandsons.

In the meantime, William Patterson's son, George, inherited Springfield in 1824. He built up an impressive farm and specialized in raising stock. The estate's famed Devon cattle were originally imported from England in 1817 and were said to be the first herd of its type in the United States.

By the time George's daughter, Florence, had inherited Springfield in 1870, the mansion was a show place. Flower beds were laid out in front of the house, and magnolia, pecan and linden trees shaded the lawn. The socially elite from Baltimore, Annapolis and Washington D.C. were often seen at the parties and receptions there.

Though unconfirmed, these are thought to be the ruins of Sykes' cotton factory. Photograph courtesy of St. Barnabas Church.

The Howard County Cotton Factory

In 1845, James Sykes built the Howard County Cotton Factory and for about 10 years employed 200 workers. Houses were built nearby, many on the Howard County side of the river. In 1857, Sykes had monetary problems and was forced to sell out.

During the Civil War, Union soldiers camping near Sykesville confiscated the machinery belting to use for shoe soles, temporarily stopping all work.

After Sykes, the factory was operated sporadically by three different owners until the 1868 flood. The cotton factory ruins were finally destroyed by fire in the early 1900s.

The Civil War and Sykesville

According to local folklore, Sykesville was a stop on the underground railroad, traveling from the Shenandoah Valley to Baltimore. Besieged by the North and the

South, troops from both sides made raids on the railroad town. A unit of General J.E.B. Stuart's Confederate cavalry burned the bridge and tore up the tracks and telegraph lines, while Union troops (mentioned above) halted production at the cotton factory.

Iron and Copper Mining

Mineral deposits were known to exist in southeastern Carroll County since before the Revolution. And, in 1849, Isaac Tyson, Jr., a well-known Maryland metallurgist, opened the Springfield iron mine on the Patterson estate. Surprisingly, at a 60 foot depth, copper was discovered. The year that Isaac Tyson died, 1861, besides iron, the mine produced copper in excess of 1,700 tons.

The mine continued to be worked for eight more years, until 1869 when Tyson's heirs were unable to renegotiate a lease renewal. Vindictively, they made sure that the mine would cave in when they left. Though the heirs had hoped that no one would ever be able to work the site again, it was reopened in 1881 for the mining of magnetic ore.

James Tyson and the Elba Furnace

Just two years before Issac Tyson began working his mine, his son, James, opened a steam and water charcoal furnace. It was 1847, and iron mining in both Frederick and Howard Counties, as well as Carroll, was going strong. By 1861, the furnace, about a mile southeast of Sykesville, was producing about 4,000 tons of car wheel iron.

The Patapsco River that supplied power for Sykes' cotton mill was also the source of power for the Elba Furnace, and relations between the two mills were occasionally strained.

James Tyson's wife, Elizabeth, gives us a glimpse of the problems in a letter dated 1851 (from Tyson Family Manuscripts, MS. 2107; Manuscripts Division; Maryland Historical Society Library).

> ...The country is parched for want of rain; the river is very low, so that the furnace has to stop for two or three hours every evening after Old Sykes shuts his dam off until it spills and runs over. He built a dam against all James could do who told him it was not legal and now I am only waiting to feel a decisive inconvenience from it and will sue him.
>
> It is a miserable neighborhood. All the people hate each other, at least the landed proprietors and even the vestry!!

The flood of 1868 wiped out the furnace and it was never rebuilt. At this point, the iron and copper industries in Maryland were already declining because of the discovery of mineral deposits in the Lake Superior region.

Boxing in Sykesville

James Tyson also received local fame when he participated in a "sparring exhibition" in Sykesville in November, 1857. One of James' friends in Baltimore writes to him and describes what he heard about the event.

"I understand indirectly," the friend writes, "that there was a sparring match at Sykesville between a young man by the name of Tyson and an older man. Our reporter (who I think was on the spot) goes on to state there were a number of persons present and several rounds were fought. It was considered that Tyson got the best of it tho' he was knocked down several times, he succeeded in puffing the old man's eye in the morning." (From the Tyson Family Manuscripts, see above.)

The Flood of 1868

The flood effectively wiped out the town on the flat land south of the river. Railroad bridges and tracks, buildings, and acres of corn and oat crops were washed away. The stone hotel built by Sykes and later owned by a John Grimes was destroyed. It was ironic that Grimes, who had been against the building of St. Joseph's Catholic Church in 1867 (no. 2 on Tour 1), fled across the river with his family to that building for safety. The Zimmerman and Schultz store that housed the post office was another flood victim. Their iron safe was lost and never recovered. The store was later rebuilt.

The mill workers, who had remained in Sykesville after the 1857 closing of the Howard County Cotton factory, fled to the steeper north bank with only the clothes on their backs. When it finally stopped raining, they rooted through the mud trying to salvage anything useful. John Berry, who later built the town's only hotel after the flood destroyed the Sykes Hotel, dried out boards to make a temporary shelter for his family.

The safe, higher side of the river was boxed in on three sides by hills, but there was only a limited space for rebuilding. Today the businesses and homes are highly concentrated in that small bowl-like area that hugs the railroad and the river. The flatter land on the south bank in Howard County has had little development.

The Sykesville that grew up after the flood of 1868. Photograph courtesy of Orlando V. Wootten.

Groveland and Susanna Warfield
Life around Sykesville in the Mid-1800s

Groveland was the name of the country estate of Baltimore merchant George Frazier Warfield in 1834, but it was Warfield's daughter, Susanna, who put Groveland on the map. She was responsible for Warfield College and initiated the formation of the St. Barnabas Church (see no. 68 on Tour 2 for more detail).

As the family's unmarried daughter, Susanna (b. 1797, d. 1890) was the hostess and caretaker for her elderly parents. Upon their death, she became the mistress of Groveland.

Susanna gives us a taste of life around Sykesville in the mid-1800s through her diaries (which are now located at the Maryland Historical Society). An industrious woman, much of her time was spent in household duties such as cleaning and sewing, in supervising the servants and in the building of an icehouse. During the winter months, she had to see that ice blocks were cut from the frozen pond and placed in the icehouse where dairy products were stored.

For recreation, Susanna would walk along the railroad tracks, read, practice the piano or guitar, write in her diary, work on her will, and entertain guests. Occasionally she went by train to Baltimore where she would stay in a boarding house, shop and visit friends.

Church was also important to Susanna. Before the building of St. Barnabas, she attended Holy Trinity Church in Eldersburg, but it was a long trip and in bad weather she would have to stay home. She also spent a part of her Sundays in teaching the slave children at Groveland their catechism, as well as reading.

At her death, at age 93, Susanna left fifty acres of Groveland and the buildings to the Episcopal Diocese of Maryland to be used as the Warfield College for boys.

Warfield College

The four-year college preparatory school was established in 1894. The stone buildings could accommodate thirty boarders, and in the 1898-99 school year, twenty boys were on the roster. The school boasted a football team (11 players and 3 substitutes), a literary society and a dramatic society.

In the school's prospectus for that year, boarding students were asked to bring 6 napkins, 1 napkin-ring, 1 clothes-bag, 1 Bible, 1 Prayer Book and 1 hymnal along with "plain and substantial clothing." (A copy of this prospectus is housed at the Maryland Historical Society.) Besides basic math and English, there were classes in German, Latin, and Greek languages; in Sacred Studies; and in Greek and Roman History.

At the end of the year, prizes were given for Neatness in the Dormitory; for Perfect Yearly Record in Deportment and Punctuality; and for Perfect Recitation of the Catechism. Of course, there were prizes for scholarship and character, too.

The Springfield Institute

Predating even Warfield College, the first organized school in Sykesville was the Springfield Academy, incorporated by officers of Springfield Presbyterian Church in 1838. The school was housed in the church and run with varying degrees of success by the residing ministers. In fact, a seminary is listed there on an 1862 map.

But it wasn't until 1878 that the well-known Springfield Institute was organized. Several prominent Sykesville citizens, including George Patterson and Stephen T.C. Brown (the father of Frank Brown — for more on him, see below entry), agreed to ask their new pastor to form a school. It was an instant success.

Frank Brown, in 1882, donated about four acres of ground across the street from the church as a permanent school site. With a $5,000 contribution from Mrs. George Patterson, a three-story frame building with a mansard roof was built. In its heyday, 1878 to 1893, the school had nearly 60 boarding and day students. The school closed about 1900, and for a while the building was used as a Christian Co-ed day school. It was later sold and eventually torn down. For a more detailed account of the history of the institute, see Thelma C. Wimmer's **The Springfield Institute 1878-1900** available at the Carroll County Historical Society.

Public Education

The success of the Springfield Institute in the late 1800s overshadowed the public school system in Sykesville. However, an 1877 map shows a school near what is now Spout Hill Road. By 1891, a Westminster newspaper noted that the Carroll County Board of Education approved a new school in Sykesville because of the dilapidated condition of the old one. The board purchased a one-half acre plot for the new building.

The new school was probably the two story, brick structure that many residents remember as the first school at the corner of Springfield Avenue and what is now Jeroby Road. There were four classrooms, a library and a principal's office.

Students from town could walk to school. But farm children had to drive a horse and buggy, and "parking" was limited. One resident remembers leaving his horse at his aunt's house in Sykesville. On snowy days, a sled was used instead of a wagon or buggy.

In the early 1900s, the school served students through the 8th grade. If a student wanted a high school education, he had to board the train for either Mt. Airy or Ellicott City. Eventually, upper level courses were offered and, by 1923, the school had a complete high school program.

By the early 20s, the small school was overflowing with students. The elementary grades were located on the second floor of a commercial building on Main Street, and portable classrooms dotted the field behind the building. In the main structure, which had no conveniences, the science class installed electric lights.

The construction of a new, larger school, next to the old one, was started in 1930 and finally completed in 1936. The old school was demolished. During the next few

The first public schoolhouse in Sykesville. Courtesy of William Frederick Church.

years, there were a number of additions to the new building including elementary school rooms, a home economics section, a cafeteria and an auditorium.

On Wednesday night, April 17, 1957, Sykesville High School burned. At the time, Sykesville did not have a public water supply, and the fire trucks could not get water to the blaze quickly enough to prevent major damage.

A new high school was built and opened in January 1959. In 1968, when the Carroll County Board of Education decided to consolidate Mt. Airy and Sykesville High Schools, the Sykesville building was converted into a middle school. Now secondary students attend either Liberty or South Carroll High School.

Frank Brown's Springfield

Rolling meadow land for cattle grazing, fields of wheat, corn, blue grass, clover and timothy, as well as hundreds of acres of timber and rich mineral deposits, made the Springfield Estate one of the most desirable farms in the county. By 1880, when Frank Brown (b. 1846, d. 1920) purchased the land from his cousin, the late Florence Patterson Carroll, the estate was the biggest dairy farm in the area.

Beside the mansion, there were about 100 outbuildings on the property, including a blacksmith shop and a mill for grinding the grain. The estate was surrounded by 12 miles of post and rail fences in addition to the fenced fields inside the estate. Maintenance on the boundary markers alone kept one man busy all year long. Many of the roads on the estate were also macadamized.

Frank Brown — Governor of Maryland from 1892 to 1896. Photograph courtesy of the Sykesville Historic Preservation Commission.

Farming, for Frank Brown, was only one of many interests. He had grown up on an estate near Sykesville called "Brown's Inheritance." His father, Stephen T.C. Brown, was one of the foremost agriculturists of the day, and it was hoped that the son would follow in his father's footsteps.

Frank, however, had other ideas. He left for Baltimore early in his career, tempted by the city's business and political opportunities. Eventually, he became Baltimore's postmaster and served as Maryland's governor from 1892 till 1896.

For a short time after he acquired Springfield, Brown generated a flurry of building projects in Sykesville. He awarded contracts for houses to local builders, built several streets, and planned a resort hotel (no. 65 on Tour 2).

He lost interest in Springfield after his wife died in 1895, and a year later, sold 728 acres of the estate to the State of Maryland for a hospital for the mentally ill.

The Sykesville Herald   [1913-1983]

By 1913, Wade H.D. Warfield, Sykesville's business magnate, was spreading the word — the railroad town was the up and coming community of south Carroll County, and it needed its own newspaper.

Three men in Baltimore, publishers of a free distribution paper called The Baltimore Budget, heard the call. David W. Dean, manager; Major Albert M. Hall, editor (and Dean's father-in-law); and William Samuel Church, the shop foreman, must have spent many hours weighing the pros and cons of a move to a small, rural town. The heavy press equipment would have to be hauled to Sykesville, and there were very few cars or trucks in 1913. The newspaper would have to start from scratch with new subscribers, advertisers and printing customers for the job shop.

The Sykesville Herald printing press being removed from the Arcade building in 1964. Photograph courtesy of William Frederick Church.

Despite the problems, the men decided to take advantage of the opportunity. Moving the equipment to the second floor of the Arcade Building (no. 14 on Tour 1) turned out to be the least of their worries. J. Edwin Hood of Sykesville operated one of the first large trucks in the town and was a natural choice for the job. The newspaper arrived and remained based in that building for 51 years, and in 1964 moved to the old Telephone Exchange building on Springfield Avenue (no. 57 on the Tour 2).

The first issue was published on September 18, 1913 and consisted of eight pages. The subscription price was $1 a year, payable in advance.

By 1918, the founders needed financial help, and a group of local business and professional people formed a stock company. At various times, the controlling interest in the Herald company was held by Wade H.D. Warfield, Frank B. Beasman, and William Samuel Church. The paper had finally won its place in the community.

During its 70 years of operation, the Herald used three different types of printing, reflecting the major eras of the printing industry. In those early years, the type was set by hand. Each letter was on a separate piece of metal and had to be placed upside down and in reverse in a rectangular metal strip.

It took several days to set the type for the paper's printing on Thursdays. Then on Friday and Saturday the typesetters had to disassemble the type and place each letter back into its slot in the type cases. On Mondays, the process began again for the next edition.

In 1956, Fred Church, then owner and editor, transferred the mechanical operation to Stromberg Publications in Ellicott City. For the next five years the paper was set in "hot type" with an entire line or strip of metal being set and cast by machine. In 1961, Stromberg switched to "cold type," and the Herald became one of the first papers in Maryland to be printed by the offset method.

The newspaper's accounts of local people and activities kept interest in the community alive. The Herald's December 11, 1913 edition, for example, told readers that the massive oak timbers passing through the Sykesville railroad yards were destined for the construction of the Panama Canal.

In another instance, the Herald saved the day for many state workers during the depression when President Roosevelt declared a Bank Holiday (March 6, 1933). The job shop was asked to print scrip which was used as money for the three state payrolls in Sykesville — at Springfield and Henryton Hospitals, and the State Roads Shop.

During the major newspaper strike in 1970, the Herald and other small weekly newspapers provided readers with extra coverage. The Herald even broke the story of Coach Don Shula's move from the Baltimore Colts football team to the Miami Dolphins.

However, it was the local stories that grabbed the community's attention... and sometimes wrecked the newspaper's schedule. For example: By 2 a.m. on Thursday, April 18, 1957, Fred Church had just laid out that week's edition of the

Sykesville High School after the fire of 1957. **Photograph courtesy of William Frederick Church.**

paper and had gone to bed. The phone call came about an hour later. Sykesville High School was burning. He rushed to the scene, then decided to scrap the stories on the front page and replace them with the fire story. He was barely finished by 8 a.m., when he had to leave and take the copy to Ellicott City for printing.

Church spent 42 years with the Herald, first in the print shop and later as editor, manager, and owner. He sold the newspaper to Stromberg in 1971, but kept the job printing operation.

Eventually, the paper was sold to Landmark Communications which discontinued publication. The final edition was dated Wednesday, December 28, 1983.

Roads and Bridges

Roads in the 1880s, especially in small country towns, were often hazardous at best, and in Sykesville there seemed to be a standing joke about strangers who first encountered the road system. According to the Democratic Advocate, a newspaper of the time, "All appear delighted with the scenery and society of this section but the public roads generally paralyzes them. 'Why do you leave those large stones in the middle of the road?' a stranger asked. 'To remind us that life is uncertain,'" was the reply.

Roads in Sykesville about this time were built privately, and store owners kept the sections in front of their businesses more or less in repair.

Sykesville in 1929. The bridge and much of the railroad tracks were washed away by Hurricane Agnes, but the Sykesville Station, seen in the center of the photograph, stands to this day. Courtesy of Orlando V. Wootten.

The bridge at the end of Main Street, by the B & O Station, links Sykesville to Howard County. It has played its own erratic role in the history of the town. In 1894, the Toledo Bridge Company of Ohio built a substantial iron bridge to replace a wooden structure that had washed away. Of course, a town beside a river has always had to consider the possiblity of flooding, and later residents recall state road crews cutting down trees from nearby woods to strengthen the underside of the bridge. Until the Route 32 by-pass was built in 1968, this bridge served as the main link between Sykesville and Howard County.

No amount of preparation could stand up against Hurricane Agnes which struck in 1972. The bridge, as well as the railroad tracks along the river, was washed away. The main part of Sykesville was covered with water and several buildings suffered structural damage.

However, there was a more longlasting damage done while a new bridge was being built. Howard County residents, who had previously come to Sykesville via the bridge to shop, would not drive the extra miles to cross the river on the Rt. 32 by-pass and swing back into the town. They found other shopping areas, and many never returned to Sykesville once the new bridge was built.

A New Beginning

It is hard to imagine that Sykesville used to be the commercial center of South Carroll County. But, as you take the tours in this book, try to picture stores that once offered the latest in clothing, groceries, and agricultural and building supplies. Sykesville was a hot spot in entertainment, too — bowling, silent and later talking movies, roller skating, local plays, debating contests, and a variety of church sponsored festivities were all available to the local townspeople.

In those earlier days on Saturday nights, Sykesville's economy received its strongest boosts. Until World War II, merchants knew that the bulk of their business for the week would be done from 6 p.m. to 11 p.m. on that evening.

But, times changed and many of the commercial interests moved to the Liberty Road/Eldersberg area. Sykesville and its Main Street were left behind.

Fortunately, the last few years have seen a reversal in that trend, and Main Street and the downtown area are planning for an active future. In 1983, the Town's Planning Commission initiated a revitalization program that has had impressive results. First among their concerns was the sixty percent business vacancy rate. In the last four years, businesses have become involved in the town's revitalization, and, as of 1987, the occupancy rate has grown to nearly one hundred percent.

One of the most significant changes in downtown ownership will be the town's purchase of the railroad station previously owned by the Chessie System, and now owned by CSX. The station, the symbol of Sykesville's economic prosperity and stability, will be purchased through a public-private partnership. The interior of the building will be refurbished and opened to the public.

One of the most basic improvements to the downtown area — and one of which most people are unaware since it is not visible — is the storm water pipe system which was laid on the west side of Main Street to carry off storm water. Before this 54" diameter pipe was laid, a make-shift open ditch ran underneath the businesses located on the west side of the street to carry water to the Patapsco River.

Other future plans for Sykesville include re-landscaping with a park along the river, new businesses and parking areas. There are currently two special events that bring newcomers and longtime residents together in community activites. In June, the town sponsers an arts festival featuring hand-picked crafts people who display their unique creative wares along Main Street. And, on the first Saturday in October, **Sykesville Day**, the town's oldest festival, annually draws visitors from all over Carroll, Howard and Baltimore Counties. The festival's variety of activities include train or trolley rides, Civil War reenactments, local tours, craft shows, and live entertainment.

People move to Sykesville and south Carroll County because of the area's traditional values and semi-rural ambiance. Perhaps this is Sykesville's most

A Civil War reenactment during "Sykesville Day" of 1985.   Photograph courtesy of the Sykesville Historic Preservation Commission.

important asset. In 1980, the town had a population of 1,712 people; in 1986, there were 2,700 residents, and Jim Schumacher, the Town Manager, estimates that in 1990, when the town will call a halt to residential growth, the population will be 3,500.

Sykesville, like the tortoise of that famous race, has proven to be a survivor, and, no doubt, will be a winner. Residents, businesspeople and town officials want to preserve the turn-of-the-century buildings and keep the small-town atmosphere alive. Then when future generations look into the past to discover their beginnings, Sykesville's place in history will be assured.

Map II — Lower Main Street, Sykesville

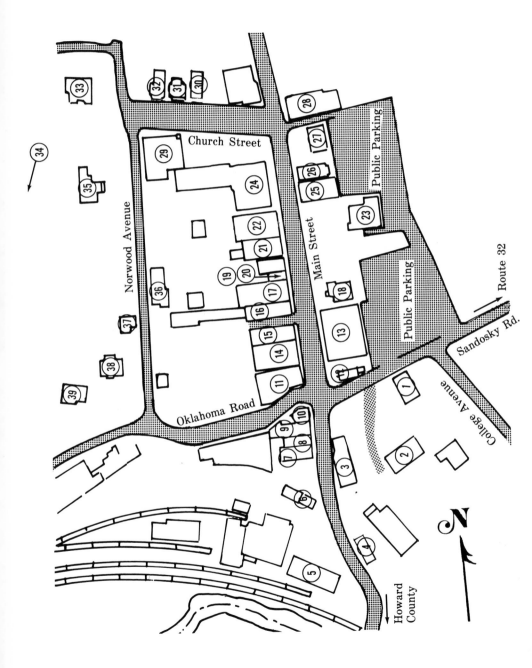

Tour 1
A Walking Tour of Main Street, Sykesville

"God dropped Main Street right out of heaven" — at least that is what town resident Lillian Brown remembers her father having said about Sykesville of the late 1800s and early 1900s. And since the town was the center of many people's lives at that time, for them, he may have been right.

The railroad linked the town to other commercial centers with passenger and freight service. Farmers clogged the streets with wagon loads of grain and other produce. Baltimoreans flocked to Sykesville's farms and boarding houses during the summer to escape the city's heat.

In fact, a June 1884 newspaper notes that there were five hundred more applicants for lodging in the area than could be supplied. By July the appetite of the summer boarders, who were eating two fried chickens a day, had become a local joke. "If Sykesville grows in popular favor," wrote the Democratic Advocate, "we will have to apply for a law for better protection of poultry."

Merchants found ready customers and numerous opportunities to dabble in various business ventures. Frank Brown (later one of Maryland's governors) wanted to build a resort hotel; the local undertaker sold candy as a sideline; and the postmaster had a confectionery shop in the post office room and also made bricks in another location.

By 1911, Main Street was a center of business and pleasure for south Carroll County farmers and residents. It was considered one of the two commercial centers of Carroll county (Westminster was the other one). There was a grain elevator and flour mill, lumber and coal yards, and stores bulging with agricultural supplies. There were also department stores and grocery markets, a bank and other service shops, including a blacksmith and a wheelwright, harness and shoemakers, barbershops, and even pool halls.

Prosperity continued into the 40s with the town boasting of two car dealerships, a theater and bowling alley.

Then, Sykesville's Main Street began a gradual decline reminiscent of main streets in other small towns across the country. Improved transportation and new shopping centers on the periphery of Baltimore seduced business away from Sykesville. The main highway through the town, Route 32, was rerouted to the outskirts in 1968; the flood of 1972 temporarily washed out the bridge into Sykesville from Howard County (see Roads and Bridges, pg. 13); and the Post Office was moved from Main Street nearer to the rerouted highway.

Despite its shove to a spot off the beaten track, Sykesville is far from being a ghost town. The historic district was entered on the National Register of Historic Places in 1985; local officials are in the process of buying the railroad station and hope to restore it as a tourist attraction; and the town has plans to lure the tourist trade as well as additional businesses.

The focus of the Sykesville Historic District is the two block commercial area of Main Street from the B & O station to Spout Hill Road. Most of the two- and three-story commercial, residential and church buildings were constructed between ca. 1850 and ca. 1925.

As you tour, be assured that businesses welcome visitors, but please respect the privacy of homes and apartments in the area.

(1) **707 Sandosky Road — The Sandosky Building.**

In 1899, a young farmer with a mechanical bent set up a farm equipment, repair and furniture store. Pennington Bennett carried parlor and bedroom suits, chiffoniers, wardrobes and cooking and heating stoves, as well as farm binders and mowers, spring tooth harrows, wagons and gasoline engines. A trucking company has also had its home here.

In 1981, the Sandosky Contracting Company remodeled the building which is now used for offices and apartments. The company owns only the building. The surrounding land is owned by St. Joseph's Catholic Church.

(2) **St. Joseph's Catholic Church.**

Construction on the stone, gable-roofed church began in 1867. Prior to this time, mass was said in the home of Dr. Orrelana Owings who had moved to Sykesville in 1852. In 1865, he gave land for a church building.

By then, work in the copper and iron mines had attracted several hundred Catholic families. And, in February of 1867, Catholic newspapers described the workers as

mostly "poor laboring men... able to contribute but little (to a building fund)."
Fellow Catholics in Baltimore, eager to help out, gave a concert of Sacred
Music — tickets were twenty-five cents a piece — to raise money for the structure. In
August 1867, the cornerstone of the church was laid.

Stone for construction was hauled from Dr. Owings' estate by ox carts. Services
were held in the building before the roof was put up, and parishioners sat on soap and
starch boxes during the mass.

There is no certain date for the completion of the church. The rear wall collapsed
before the roof was constructed, and the builder left town — never to be seen again.
It was not until September 7, 1879 that the church was finally dedicated. However, it
is said that during the flood of 1868 people living on the Howard County side of the
Patapsco took refuge in the completed sections of the church.

Through the years, the building has been improved or renovated several times. In
1883, a belfry, a gilded cross and a bell weighing 275 lbs. were added. Later, the
pot-bellied stoves and coal oil lamps were replaced by a furnace and electricity along
with other interior modernizations.

A new church building on Freedom and Liberty Roads was built in 1964. However,
mass is still celebrated regularly at the old church in Sykesville.

③ St. Barnabas Episcopal Parish House.

This two-story gable roofed meetinghouse is a good example of 19th century stone
building in the Patapsco valley. The structure is three bays deep and five bays wide
on the South end, and two deep and two wide on the North end. It was built by Dr.
Owings as a store for his son-in-law in 1865 and sold to another merchant, John
McDonald, in 1868. It was one of the few buildings in Sykesville to survive the flood
that year.

As a general store in the late 1800s and early 1900s, it sold everything the family of
the time needed. On the first floor were barrels of flour, sugar and salt, underwear,
hats, caps, feed, coal and bolts of gingham and muslin. Loose loaves of bread were
not wrapped and were placed in wooden crates. However, bread was not a big

seller — most of the baking in those years was done at home. Storage rooms were packed with potatoes, coal oil and feed.

Originally, steep curving steps at the end of the building (on the train station side) led to the second floor. Here, ladies' and men's shoes and boots were sold. It was also used as a storage area.

In 1939, the Volunteer Fire Department purchased and renovated the old stone store. When they moved to their new building on Main Street in 1949, the building was sold to the Episcopal Church.

(4) **Farm and Home Service, Inc., A Southern States Agency; Miller's Flea Market and Collectibles; and Schatz's Power Equipment, Inc.**

While the building which houses both the Farm and Home Service and Schatz's Power Equipment is fairly new, having been built in the 1970s, the Miller's Flea Market building is much older. At one time it was a busy gas station. Below the floor, there is still an open bay over which cars were driven so that repairmen could work underneath them.

(5) **The B & O Railroad Station.**

Although the railroad was completed to Sykesville in 1831, the town did not get an official station until 1884.

The Sykesville station, like many other B & O stations of the time, is attributed to Baltimore architect E. Francis Baldwin, and was part of a general station-building program. All supposedly designed by Baldwin, each station has its own unique look, while still sharing stylistic similarities. They combined to form one of the most attractive groups of stations on any railroad.

The station is a Queen Anne structure built of Baltimore pressed brick and red mortar with sandstone sills and lintels and a slate roof. The center portion of the building is two-stories high and has 5 small rooms in the upper story. On the ground floor are two waiting rooms, a ticket and telegraph office, and a freight room.

The building has multiple gables featuring decorative stick and spindle work. The roof projects 6 feet and is supported by ornamental brackets. The windows on the upper story are bordered by small panes of cathedral glass. When it was built, the station was painted in red and chocolate with sage green trimmings and was touted as the only depot on the line that had a vestibule in the rear.

The station was closed when passenger service was discontinued in 1949. However, the freight office remained open, handling freight for Springfield Hospital Center and other customers in the area. Finally, that office, too, was closed in the early 1980s, however, carloads are still occasionally delivered to the Farm and Home Services company.

(6) **7610 Main Street — Captain's Quarters Seafood and Produce Market.**
The First Modern Firehouse.

According to local lore, the wooden, two-story, front gabled structure was originally built as a salt shed in the mid-1800s. It had four walls and a roof, but no solid floor.

The railroad tracks which run along the north side of the building were part of the original train route through the town. However, from 1837 on, the B & O was constantly straightening and realigning the sharp curves of the original route. In his history of the B & O, **The Impossible Challenge**, Herbert H. Harwood, Jr. wonders if this building could have been an early station for the town. So far there is no evidence to support that theory.

By 1933, the building was vacant.

In 1934, when this photograph was taken, the Sykesville Volunteer Fire
Company had been in operation for only a few months. Courtesy of Orlando V.
Wootten.

The Sykesville-Freedom District Fire Department

On a July evening in 1933, a fire was discovered at the Hugg Mansion just over the
river in Howard County (no. 69 on Tour 2). The nearest fire company was in Ellicott
City. They were too late to save the mansion.

Sykesville residents realized that the town was too dependent on other volunteer
fire companies. The town's earlier fire equipment, circa 1900, was useless (no. 36 on
this tour). Almost immediately the campaign began for a Sykesville Volunteer Fire
Department. By the end of the year, the newly formed company had a 500-gallon
pumper truck. During the first months of operation, the firemen did not have helmets
or boots. And for several years, before the advent of safety glass, the fire engine was
not allowed to have a windshield. The cold bit through the firemen when they had to
rush to a fire on a long winter's night.

This dilapidated frame building was offered as a fire house. Volunteers spent
evenings pouring concrete and restoring the old structure. The ground floor was used
to house the fire engine, and the second floor became a meeting room. The building
was used as a fire station until 1939, when it was replaced by the general store
building across the street (no. 3 on this tour).

The Fire Next Door

In October of 1937, flames shot through the roof of the food market beside the fire
station. When the firemen tried to pipe water from the nearby Patapsco River, mud
and silt clogged up the fire plug. Wind swept the fire out of control. The food market,
a hardware store, a barber shop, a pool hall and second-story apartments were
destroyed. The brick building on the far corner was not damaged. With the exception
of the market, the row of stores were rebuilt.

(7) **7606 Main Street — Maria's Restaurant.**

If you walked into this two-story building at the turn of the century, you would find the Post Office and Postmaster Asa Hepner's tobacco and confectionery store. You could also buy crochet and embroidery cotton from Mrs. Hepner. There was a music store, too. Hepner was appointed as a third class postmaster during President William McKinley's term (1897 - 1901). A few years earlier, Hepner manufactured bricks with another businessman. A newspaper report says he was so delighted with his first kiln of bricks that "he carried a hot brick around the village to exhibit it."

After the fire of 1937, the structure was rebuilt and at various times has been used as a tobacco store and pool parlor as well as a hardware store.

(8) **7604 Main Street — Remember This.**

For fifty years, until 1983, this one-story building was the home of "Happy" Keeney's Barber Shop. He was a town mayor, as well as a chief of the volunteer fire department. If a customer was in the middle of having a haircut and the alarm sounded, Happy would leave. But, the customer could return later and Happy would finish the job for free. Happy was also known to raise pigeons, and at least one person has memories of them flying about the shop while Happy cut hair.

For short periods of time, Happy also had a pool room and a pet shop. But his first love was fishing. Sykesville residents who needed a fishing partner knew that Happy needed little coaxing to get him to close up shop and head for the pond.

(9) **7602 Main Street — Betty's Country Store.**

The frame structure with dormer windows was built in 1878. It has the original storefront, complete with colored-glass transoms over the entranceway and the display windows. Tenants have included a barbershop, a pool room and a plumbing business.

(10) **7600 Main Street — Lloyd Helt Jr.'s law office.**

Architecture in small towns is often a combination of styles that have been popular in larger cities. This two-story brick building, constructed in the early 1900s, has a flat

roof, parapet, arched windows and stone trim. It combines features of the Georgian Revival, Romanesque and Neoclassical styles and was designed by Sykesville's resident architect, J. H. Fowble (no. 33 on this tour).

The history of the building in terms of its tenants is not quite as exciting as its architecture. It was built as the First National Bank. But the financial institution went out of business after about five years.

Other businesses which have set up shop here include the telephone exchange (no. 57 on Tour 2) a drug store, a liquor store and a barbershop. It was often empty between tenants.

⑪ **7568 Main Street — Consolidated Stationers, Inc.**
A former General Merchandise Store.

In the late 1800s and early 1900s, E. M. Mellor's general store was the largest in town. The two-story, frame building with a bracketed cornice boasted more than

10,000 square feet of floor space. If you were shopping here in 1910, you would find ready-made clothing, groceries, rugs, dry goods, notions, and 5- and 10-cent counters.

It continued as a general store under different owners until the 1960s.

⑫ A former Gas Station.

This hip-roof brick structure was built as a station about 1920 and was in use until the mid-1970s.

⑬ 7565 Main Street — The Moose Lodge.

Instead of a building, picture a wide expanse of rolling green lawn bordered by a thick private hedge. These grounds effectively framed and isolated the McDonald house (now the Town House, no. 23 on this tour) from the bustle of Main Street.

The commercial structure was built about 1925 by Edwin Hood and became known locally as the Hood Building. On the ground floor, at various times, there was a grocery store, offices, a movie theater and the post office. The second floor has always been apartments.

⑭ 7566 Main Street — Greenberg Publishing Company.
Formerly the Arcade Building.

Built in the early 1900s, the Arcade is a three-story, three-bay, buff-colored brick building. It was designed by local architect, J. H. Fowble, to have a store on each side of the passage way. On the ground floor, at various times, there were men's haberdashery shops, an A & P store and a Post Office.

From 1913 to 1963, one side of the second floor was the first home of the local newspaper, The Sykesville Herald (see pg. 11 and no. 57 on Tour 2). Opposite were dental and insurance offices. A masonic lodge occupied the entire third floor.

⑮ 7564 Main Street — The Maryland National Bank.

A banking institution has always been in this building. It was organized as the Sykesville National Bank in 1901 and built by Fowble.

Originally the building had a two-bay facade of orange brick with terra cotta detailing. However, by the late 50s, a modernization trend was sweeping the country.

Though now almost hidden, the stylish Romanesque arches can still be made out behind the metal grillwork.

A polished granite veneer was applied to the first story and the upper story was covered by a metal grille. If you look closely through the grille, you can see the original arches.

It was the second floor of the bank that attracted most Sykesville residents. They gathered in this large room for church plays, debating contests, and dances. It was also the local movie theater. A piano on one side of the room provided accompaniment to the silent films.

16 7558 Main Street — Former offices of Wade H.D. Warfield.

At one time this three-story brick building was the headquarters of the man who powered Sykesville's commercial growth in the early 20th century. In 1889, Wade H.D. Warfield, at the age of 25, brought his dream of business success to Main Street. He had grown up nearby, on the large estate of "Chihuahua," now called "Raincliffe" (no. 78 in Other Historic Spots), and was familiar with the potential of the little town on the railroad.

His lumber and coal yard, located behind the building, became one of the largest in the state. He even had a private switch that ran from the B & O railroad to his property. Gondolas on the elevated rails emptied coal into storage bins. Lumber, bricks, tile and other building materials were also stacked in the yard.

The structure on Main Street served as the builder's hardware and supply store, storage and office space. It has a rusticated granite facade on the first story. The two upper stories are of buff brick, and the broad three-part windows have a splayed brick arch with granite keystone and impost blocks. Note the modillioned cornice of pressed metal at the roof line.

By 1910, Warfield had also constructed a large grain elevator (still standing) and a flour mill (no longer in existence). He was producing 100 barrels of "Cook's Delight" flour a day.

In addition to his other enterprises, he built the Arcade, was president of the Sykesville National Bank and owned the town of Marriottsville which was rich in mineral deposits.

From the early 30s on, the Warfield building has had several owners including the Morrow Company which manufactured wood products such as crates and pallets. They went out of business about 1970 and the building has been vacant ever since. (Ed. note: Having cleaned and re-painted the building, the new owner, Charles B. Mullins, hopes to bring in new businesses.)

(17) **7556 Main Street — McDougall's Pharmacy.**

The building was constructed in the mid-1950s for use as a clothing store. About 10 years later, it became the pharmacy. Originally a boarding house was on this site.

(18) **7557 Main Street   [private residence].**

(19) **7554 Main Street — Stevens' Music Store; and**

(20) **7552 Main Street — Jim's Barbershop.**

Built in 1878, these two shops were one building. One half was a butcher shop, and a door in the middle led up one step to the other half which had a barbershop and confectionery store. At various times the building has also housed a plumbing shop, a dry cleaners, and a taxi service.

The frame building is two-stories high with bracketed cornices.

(21) **7550 Main Street — Harris Food Market [although the sign still says Harris, it is now owned by Parks]; 7548 Main Street — Miller's Tax Service; and 7548 Main Street — Main Street Dry Goods.**

This building, which now has signs for three businesses, used to be a single family general merchandise store. In 1901, harnessmaker John Harris probably never dreamed that his small shop would provide a livelihood for three generations.

He added groceries to his list of services in the early 1900s, and, as his daughters grew up, he expanded his stock. Margaret Harris operated the women's department store from the early teens to about 1940. The Harris shoe shop divided it from the grocery.

The last Harris family member to run the grocery store sold the business in 1983.

(22) **7546 Main Street — Think Oak.**

In the early 1900s, hats were made, by hand, to last a lifetime. And from 1903 until about 1930, the place to shop for hats in Sykesville was the millinery shop of Miss Minnie Phillinger. The frames and straw hats were shipped in by train. Miss Phillinger and her assistants trimmed the straw hats with flowers, bands and feathers, and covered the frames with velvets, silks and satins.

Other tenants of the building since the '30s have included a meat and grocery store, and a 5- and 10-cent store.

(23) **7547 Main Street — The Town House [besides housing the town offices, several rooms on the second floor have been set up as a museum.]**

This Colonial Revival house, circa 1883, used to be the home of one of Sykesville's first merchants, John McDonald. He had bought the old stone store (no. 3 on this tour) in 1868. J.H. Fowble designed this two-story house. It has a center front gable and a full-width one-story porch with a smaller center gable.

(24) **7540 Main Street — Avanta Video Distributer and Delft Blue.**

The outside of this three-story building has been radically altered over the years. But it served Sykesville's residents as a farm and home supply house or hardware-type store since the mid-1800s until only recently.

W. H. Bennett had only a small amount of stock when he started his business in about 1883. However, by 1910, he was boasting of a 15,000 square foot store in which he sold farming equipment, furniture, wall paper and paint as well as seed and fertilizers. He also added a third story and remodeled the outside.

Inside the store, the tin print ceiling was installed about 1920. These stamped, metal sheets were quite popular in commercial establishments in the late 1800s and early 1900s.

(25) **7543 Main Street — Dawson Electronics.**
Former Sykesville Firehouse.

The two-story formstone-faced building was constructed in 1949 as the third home of the fire department (also see no. 6 and no. 36 on this tour). During the dedication ceremonies in May of that year, the fire truck and crew had to respond to a fire call.

Fire came too close to home in February, 1969. The station itself caught on fire, and the engine room was heavily damaged. Two fire trucks were also destroyed.

After 34 years, the firemen voted to close this station and build a larger and more centrally-located facility at nearby Flohrville.

(26) **7541 Main Street — Hair 'N Place.**

The original brick structure was built around 1900 and was used as a lunch room on the ground floor and a residence on the second floor.

(27) **7537 Main Street — A. L. Howes, Inc.**

Originally built as a gas station in the late 1920s, this building has been redesigned and is now used as an insurance office.

(28) **7533 Main Street — Captain's Quarters Restaurant.**

In 1920, employees at this white-block building had to partially assemble the cars they sold. When the dealership ordered Fords from Detroit, the cars were sent in sections on the train. At the station, men would put the wheels on, set the bodies into the frame and tow the cars to the building to finish the assembly.

A duck pin bowling alley and a crab restaurant have also been in business at this location.

(29) **St. Paul's United Methodist Church.**

The church is set back from Main Street for a good reason. What is now the front of the building used to be the back entrance. In fact, the present site is the church's second location.

Originally the church was built in 1878 on the Howard County side of the Patapsco at approximately where St. Lukes Church on Rt. 32 stands today (no. 71 on Tour 2). It was described as a handsome stone structure with stained glass windows and a bell.

In 1889, the church was rebuilt at the present location and incorporated some of the stones, including the cornerstone, the bell and the stained glass windows from the original building. The entrance then faced Norwood Avenue.

As more merchants built on Main Street, the front was relocated. In 1903, two gable-fronted additions were built on each side of the main entrance and tied together with a pent roof. Note the decorative stickwork and imbricated shingles on the gables.

St. Paul's Church, probably shortly after the 1903 additions were made. The J. E. Norwood house (no. 35 on this tour), which has recently been renovated, can be seen on the hill behind the Church. Photograph courtesy of Orlando V. Wooten and the Sykesville Historic Preservation Commission.

In 1931, the church was renovated and remodeled. Sunday school rooms and a social hall were added. In the social hall and two of the Sunday School rooms, murals of rich, intensive hues depict the birth and growth of Methodism. They were painted by local artist Richard Bagley.

(30) **through** (32) **Church Street [private residences].**

These two-story frame houses were probably built in the late 1800s. They have the rough stone foundations common to houses of the 19th century. No. 30 (706 Church Street) and no. 32 (702 Church Street) have steeply pitched roofs and center gables. Often referred to as a center gable cottage, this type of house was popular in the late 1800s. Note the Gothic or pointed arched window in the gable on no. 32.

Norwood Avenue

Older residents remember their grandparents telling them that this street used to be the old wagon road from Sykesville to Frederick. Although the original fire station was located here, other businesses set up shop on another village road — now Main Street.

Norwood Avenue got its name, probably in the early 1900s, from J. E. Norwood who was constantly building additions on to his house (no. 35 on this tour).

(33) **7514 Norwood Avenue   [private residence].**
Former home of Sykesville architect, J. H. Fowble.

By the early 1900s, Fowble had built his own three-story frame house. An example of an asymmetrical Colonial Revival, it was described by his peers as an artistic home. The structure has a broad front porch, cross gables and a dormer window.

Fowble began his career with training from an architectural design correspondence school. By the 1890s, he was gaining a local reputation as an architect and builder. He was responsible for the Arcade, the Wade H.D. Warfield Store, both bank buildings, the present Town House and several private residences.

At Springfield State Hospital he built the Warfield Cottage, a huge three-story Colonial Revival building with a centered gable and dormer windows. He also built the two-story dining hall which features a broad full height entry porch supported with columns.

(34) Springs.

Although they are now inaccessible, behind the houses on Norwood Avenue are some of the springs which served as Sykesville's water supply until public water facilities came in 1968. However, a nearby spring is still used privately. The spring which served the B & O Railroad originated from Spout Hill; the water flowed down Main Street through a wooden pipe. The Springfield Avenue area was served by a spring located behind where the middle school is now. All of these springs are part of the underground streams that run beneath the town.

On the steep hill behind these houses is also the railroad spur which used to serve Springfield State Hospital.

(35) 7534 Norwood Avenue [private residence].

An agent for the B & O Railroad, Mr. J. E. Norwood purchased a simple three-bay two-story cottage with a flat roof in 1886 (similar to no. 39 on this tour). It didn't stay simple for long. He began a series of fanciful alterations which included a steep mansard roof, three towers, a cupola, a porch and a third story with dormer windows. Note the eave brackets on the cornice lines and the ornately carved fascia board on the porch.

The cathedral glass windows are similar to the ones in the train station where Norwood had lived previously.

Behind the house is an outbuilding, also with a tower. At one time there was a windmill atop the tower. There have been several owners who have added, and later removed, barns for chicken and egg farms. The house itself weathered much neglect and dismemberment over the years, however, it has now been restored.

(36) 7539 Norwood Avenue [private residence].
Original Firehouse, Jail and Stables.

When there was a fire in the village in the 1890s, volunteers would rush to this building. If no horses were in the stables, men would grab the tongue of the pump

wagon and haul it themselves to the blaze. Strong arms were needed to push the four long handles of the pump up and down. With hard work, maybe enough pressure could be built up to pump the water ten or twelve feet through a hose. The stables were located in the lower section of the building with the jail cells. But horses were kept there only on special occasions such as a town parade.

In 1905, a chemical fire engine was brought into Sykesville. It was a major event for the small town, and a big celebration was held to hail its arrival.

In the jail section, there were three, narrow cells with thick masonry walls, each four-and-a-half feet wide by eight feet long. Initials and the usual jail-house humor which were etched into the concrete exist to this day.

On the left side of the firehouse there used to be a narrow room with a separate roof. This area was probably used when the local judge held court.

Facing the house, the far left portion is probably not as old as the fire station. However, these walls, too, show their age since they are at least two feet thick.

Now the three sections have been remodeled into a handsome private residence. Although the entrance to the fire station has been sealed off, the outline of the large doors can still be seen. It retains the original German siding, but shingles hide the siding on the newer portion of the building.

(37) **7540 Norwood Aveune   [private residence].**

The original portion of this house was once a stable either for the firehouse or for the property next door at 7546 Norwood. It was remodeled as a residence probably about 1915 or 1920.

(38) **7546 Norwood Avenue   [private residence].**

The two-story, three bay house has a metal standing seam roof in the hipped shape and a hipped roof attic dormer. The full-width porch is supported by columns. It was probably built after the turn of the century.

(39) **718 Oklahoma Road   [private residence].**

The simple, two-story, three bay house has a flat standing seam roof and a full width porch. It appears that the original portion of the J.E. Norwood house may have looked like this structure (no. 35 on this tour).

Upper Main Street

(Note: This portion of the tour may be walked, or may be driven in conjunction with **Tour 2 — The Driving Tour.**)

(40) **7532 Main Street [Corner of Church and Main] — now apartments.**

A story is told of a Sunday morning around 1915, when a small boy slipped out of St. Paul's Church and scooted over to the car dealership on the corner of Main Street. He climbed into the front seat of a new Reo car and, breaking the sabbath peace of the worshipers, joyfully punched the horn. Our storyteller survived the punishment he received that day and grew up to become a respected citizen of the town, but the Reo and car dealership had disappeared before the 1940s.

Reos were first made in 1904 by Ransom E. Olds, who had pioneered the Oldsmobile in 1901. The Reo — which were the initials of the founder's name — was a durable and good quality car, but 1936 was its last year of production.

However, the car dealership, which also sold Chevrolets, probably was gone by the 1920s. People still remember that the repair shop was on the second floor of the building. The cars were hoisted up on a platform by a system of pulleys.

The mischievous, small boy may have had less trouble with the next two businesses which occupied this building. First, there was a clothing store, and later, Ken Barnes opened a soda fountain which also sold tobacco, jewelry and gas. Barnes

Map III — Upper Main Street, Sykesville

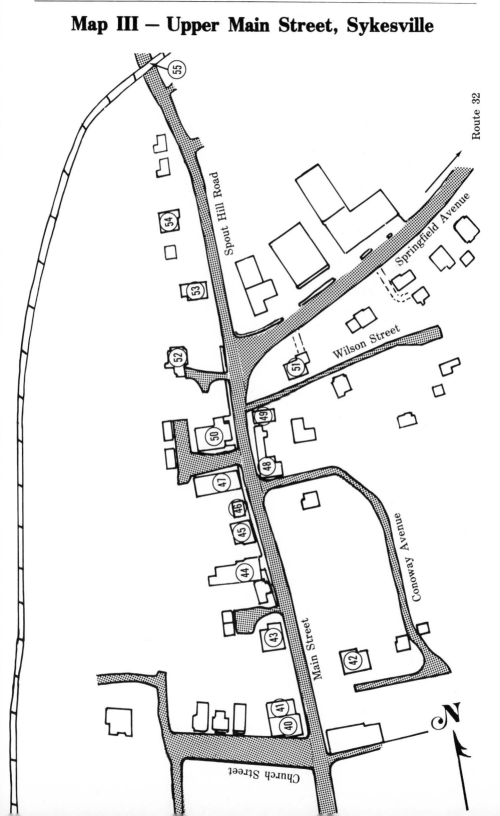

lived on the second floor over his shop.   Eventually the building was made into apartments.

(41) **7530 Main Street — The Carrollton Apartments.**

During the late 1800s, this building was known as the "Odd Fellows Hall." The fraternal organization met on the second floor, and various businesses occasionally set up shop on the first floor. Barnes' soda fountain and tobacco shop started here before moving next door. By the mid-1930s, the Odd Fellows had given up their charter. After a period of vacancy, the building was converted into apartments.

(42) **7527 Main Street   [private residence].**

This house was built in the early 1900s as the home and office of Dr. Lucas, a general practitioner. Note the concrete garage along the road which is built into the side of the hill.

(43) **7526 Main Street — Creative Ceramics on the first floor and living quarters on the second floor.**

The log wall in the entrance hall is the first clue that this building may be one of the oldest in Sykesville. An early document mentions William Baer as the owner in 1857, and his name appears at this spot on a military map of 1863. Log walls on the second floor have also been uncovered and preserved. Originally the space between these logs was filled with a mixture of sand, lime, horse hair and flat stones.

A frame addition doubled the house size in the 1880s, and a back portion was added between 1910 and 1930. The basement, which is not open to the public, is five feet high and the joists for the first floor are logs that have only one side squared off flat.

According to local lore there used to be manacles and chains in the basement, but these are said to have been removed in the 1930s. There are still train spikes and a hook in the beams. And there are rumors, which have not been verified, that the house is haunted by a friendly spirit who keeps two rooms dust free.

The building is still in the process of being renovated. A porch and bay window on the street side have been removed. Bricks from the inside fireplace have been used for the four-foot facing on the outside. In addition, the present storefront windows were the original ones used in the Arcade building.

At times the house has been used as the Methodist parsonage, a general store, a residence and the town polling center. Sykesville's Postmaster of the early 1900s, Asa Hepner, bought the building in 1888. Older Sykesville residents can remember lining up in his parlor to vote.

(44) **7522 Main Street — J & B Motors.**

Constructed in 1925, this renovated building has always been a garage.

(45) **7518 Main Street — Kevin's Katering.**

In the early 1900s, this house was the home and business of Clarence Brown, one of the three shoe and harness makers in the town. At one point, Brown even added a barber's chair in his front room. His wife also used part of the house for boarders, particularly the construction crews from the telephone company.

(46) **7516 Main Street** [private residence].

This building has been used as a combination plumbing shop and residence. Later, a barbershop was located on the north side of the front of the house.

(47) **7512 Main Street — a woodworking shop on the first floor.**

When the train brought carloads of new carriages and wagons to Sykesville in the early 1900s, many of them went to this, the R. W. Carter Building. The light vehicles were stored on the second floor. In fact, there are still double doors high on the backside of the building which led to the storage area. The carriages were hauled up to the second floor with pulleys. Carter also sold furniture and attracted customers from other parts of Carroll County and Baltimore.

About 1920, the building was sold and used for a Hudson and Essex car dealership. Hudsons were made from 1909 to 1957. The Essex, made from 1919 to

1933, has gone down in history as the first affordable car to have an enclosed body. Until 1921, most cars were open and only the luxury models were enclosed.

At other times, the building has been used for overflow public school classrooms and as a sewing factory.

The Sykesville Hotel as it appeared during its heydays in about 1912-13. Photograph courtesy of William and Rose McDonald.

(48) **7511 Main Street — now apartments.**
Formerly the Sykesville Hotel.

Wide porches meant for relaxing and telling yarns used to be one of the main features of the hotel built in the late 1860s. The three-story section of the building had a full-width, two-story porch with a railing on the second floor. The two-story section had a one-story porch with spindlework detailing.

John M. Berry built the hotel after his shop on the Howard County side of the Patapsco River had been washed away. It had a number of owners through the years. By 1910, the hotel had passed into the hands of John Weetenkamp who brought German style cooking and a well stocked bar to the Sykesville area. The hotel closed about 1920 and was made into apartments.

(49) **7509 Main Street — now apartments.**

In the early 1900s, the butcher was just as important as the grocer. Sykesville residents would make a stop here at the Jenkins Butcher Shop when they were out shopping for the week's groceries.

(50) **7508 Main Street — now apartments.**

This was the second location for the Weer Funeral Home (the business is now known as the Haight Funeral Home which relocated to Rt. 32 in Eldersburg in 1958 — for the first location, see no. 53 on this tour).

Imagine walking down to the local funeral home and buying 15 cents worth of cabbage or candy. Yet, in the early 1900s, that is just what local residents did. The undertaker, Harry Weer, had a small store in a side room of his establishment. At that time most undertakers needed a second line of employment.

The Weers lived in the rear portion of their funeral home. On busy days, they would move the furniture out of the dining room and place bodies there for viewing. Mrs. Weer would have coffee and, occasionally, a ham in the kitchen for visitors.

This house is now being renovated.

(51) **7503 Main Street [private residence].**

Picture a blacksmith and a wheelwright shop practically jutting out into the street at the curve of this lawn. In the late 1800s, it was easy for farmers to drive their horses and wagons into these two shops.

(52) **7500 Main Street [private residence].**

In the late 1800s, this was the home of a shoemaker. He made and repaired shoes in a separate one-room wooden building which has since been torn down.

(53) **7442 Spout Hill Road [private residence].**

This was the retirement home of James Weer, the undertaker.

(54) and 54A 7436 Spout Hill Road [private residence].

This house was the first location of the Weer Funeral Home. James Weer started the business in 1887 and used the small house to embalm the bodies. In a two story building in the back (no longer there), he kept the horses and the hearse. On the second floor, he built caskets out of white pine and covered the inside with gray cloth.

(55) The "Dinky Track."

Springfield State Hospital, in the early 1900s, needed some type of transportation for patients, as well as for obtaining supplies, particularly coal for the heating system. In 1908, the State of Maryland responded by laying a three-mile spur off the main B & O line. Called the "Dinky Track" by residents, the trestle rises over Spout Hill Road and a nearby house, which was there even before the track was built.

For 64 years, engines would haul coal two or three times a week to the hospital. By the early 1970s, the hospital switched to oil and the "Dinky Track" was closed down. Now, much of the track, especially the sections behind homes, is overgrown with weeds or is demolished.

Map IV — The Outskirts of Sykesville

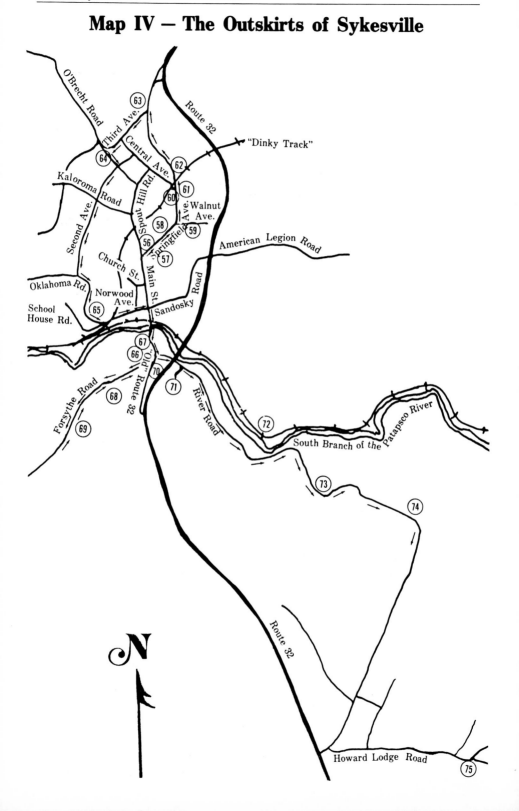

Tour 2

A Driving Tour — The Outskirts of Sykesville

While Main Street was the hub of activity and recreation for the old Sykesville area, the surrounding homes, farms, and factories were often the lifeblood for the town. This tour takes you to some of the more important of those locations. In most cases, the original structures from the past still exist, however, some are merely marked by a plaque and some simply rest in the memories of the town elders.

Many residents have graciously shared their historical discoveries, but please remember that their private residences are not open to the public.

Springfield Avenue

A bottle of Champagne, music and speeches marked the opening of Springfield Avenue in 1883. Frank Brown had decided that the new road could be built without complying with the local building requirements. He talked with several farm owners and got them to agree to a route through part of their lands. A newspaper article in 1883 stated that Mr. Brown would make the road and "spare no expense."

(56) **7448 Springfield Avenue — Dunn-Rite Pipe Furniture.**

A welcome newcomer to Sykesville, Dunn-Rite moved to Sykesville in September of 1986.

(57) **7443 Springfield Avenue — William F. Church Printing. Formerly the Telephone Exchange and the Sykesville Herald.**

By 1885, agents from the telephone company were in Sykesville hunting for subscribers to the new telephone system. According to one source, when the turn of the century came around, the telephone exchange, with its one operator, had been established in a private residence on Church Street.

However, the Church Street exchange lasted for only a short time, and the first major location for the local phone service in those early years was over the First National Bank (no. 10 on Tour 1). By 1919, the operators and switching equipment had outgrown their space at that location, and this two-story brick building was constructed. Operators manned the switchboard here around the clock until the phone company switched to the dial system in 1962.

The building was sold to Fred Church, owner of the Sykesville Herald in 1963.

The Sykesville Herald

The weekly newspaper began in the Arcade Building (no. 14 on Tour 1) in 1916, and continued to publish from there until 1964 when it moved to Springfield Avenue. For nearly seventy years, the paper was rich in community news and recorded Sykesville's prosperity as well as the changing economic patterns.

Church sold the paper in 1971 and the new owners continued operation until December 28, 1983. Fortunately for historians, microfilms of all the paper's issues are available at the museum in the Town House.

(For more detailed information on the Sykesville Herald, see page 11 in "Tales of Sykesville.")

Residences on Springfield Avenue

A look at the exterior of the private homes on Springfield Avenue shows the different trends in architecture of the last 90 years. There are about two dozen frame houses here representing a potpourri of architectural styles. Though not every house on Springfield Avenue is listed below, the ones discussed are representative of the historical importance of them all.

The "I-House" was a popular style in rural Maryland from the mid-1800s through the early 1900s. They are two-story houses, one-room in depth, and characterized by a central front-facing cross gable, a one story porch, a central entrance, and often a shed at the back. For examples of this style notice the houses at 7311, 7312 and 7327 Springfield Avenue.

The Queen Anne style was fashionable in the late 1800s. Interpretations of this sort of house can be seen at 7320 and 7332 Springfield Ave. They include the multiple gables with fishscale shingles, wrap around porches and complex massing.

In the early 1900s, Colonial Revival Houses were in vogue. 7326 and 7338 Springfield are examples of this style. Note the colored-glass sidelights and fanlight of 7338.

The "foursquare" form is a generic term that describes a two-story almost square house with a hipped roof and a central hipped dormer. It was built from the late 1800s to about 1940. Examples can be seen at 7321, 7337, and 7345 Springfield Avenue.

The "homestead" designation is another term for a front or open-gable house. It is usually a two-story with simple lines. 7322 Springfield is an example.

(58) **7406 Springfield Avenue — Long Way Bed and Breakfast.**

The huge rock formation which cuts into the hill on the front yard of this house distinguishes it from its neighbors. On that site, in the late 1800s, was a blacksmith shop. Because of the heat, smell and noise from the forge, the blacksmith had his house located far back on the property.

The front part of the house with the cross gable is an addition that was built about 1900. The back section appears to have been a small farm or tenant house and has a primitive basement similar to that of the Creative Ceramics building which was built before 1857 (no. 43 on Tour 1). A center brick fireplace separates the two parts of the building. A tunnel, which is only rumored to have existed, began at this basement and ended at that of a house lower down on Spout Hill. Slaves traveling the

underground railroad to freedom in the North were said to have been hidden there before they continued their journeys. It is believed that the tunnel still exists, although it has yet to be found.

(59) **Stone pillars at Springfield and Walnut Avenues.**

These stone gate posts marked the entrance to one of the farms surrounding Sykesville in the late 1800s. The owner was one of those who gave permission for the Avenue to be built. The posts are made from granite stringers that held the strap rail for the B & O tracks in 1831. On close inspection, the rail markings can still be seen.

(60) **7318 Springfield Avenue   [private residence].**

Wade H.D. Warfield, who initiated the commercial growth of Sykesville, lived here after he sold the family home of Chihuahua. The gable-front house has a full-width, one-story porch with decorative spindlework.

(61) **7311 Springfield Avenue   [private residence].**

Originally, the house had four rooms and was a farm tenant's lodging. A kitchen and an upstairs third bedroom were added about 1920. There is a center staircase with a room on each side, both upstairs and down. The stone foundation is at least 22 inches deep.

The house has more recently been covered with aluminum siding, but other features are original, including the front door and bell.

(62) The Millard Cooper Park 1.

This seven-acre public park has been described as one of the best developed and best built parks in the state. The stone pillars on either side of the park entrance used to mark the gateway into Springfield State Hospital.

(63) Fairhaven — A Life-Care Retirement Community.

Mention "Fairhaven," and most older Sykesville residents remember what was once a prosperous working farm and, for a short time, a dairy operation. The land was part of Frank Brown's Springfield estate, but, in 1884, it was aquired by Johnzie E. Beasman. When he married, Beasman renamed it, "Fairfields."

Large building projects in the 1880s usually attracted attention in local newspapers, and the construction at the Beasmans' new farm was no exception. Johnzie and his wife, Laura, had the existing farmhouse rebuilt into a fourteen-room, three-story mansion. Even the new barn received favorable press.

The land was used for general farming until Frank, the couple's only son, converted it to a dairy operation which he named "Fairhaven." During its heyday, in the 1930s and 40s, the dairy farm delivered milk to local customers as well as several businesses in Baltimore.

However, Frank Beasman seemed to be more interested in construction than farming. He had his own construction company, and later joined the McLean Construction Company in Baltimore, where he was President as well as Chairman of the Board. He died in July 1960 at age 71.

In his will, Frank left $3,000,000 and over three-hundred acres of Fairhaven Farm to the Episcopal Church. He asked that the money and land be used for a facility for aged men and women. The life-care retirement community opened in 1980.

The Beasman mansion, which by today's standards was no longer considered safe, and other farm buildings were eventually torn down to make room for additional facilities for the retirement complex. However, over one-third of the land is still forest, and another portion has been rented for cultivation.

A very youthful Frank Beasman. Photograph courtesy of Orlando V. Wootten.

The Beasman mansion at Fairhaven as it appeared shortly before it was torn down. Photograph courtesy of Orlando V. Wootten.

The Fairhaven Nature Trail

Fairhaven's trees and wildflowers immediately attracted Roland Ferguson, a retired forester and resident of the center, to its verdant woodlands. Unfortunately, there were too many brambles and honeysuckle bushes tangled through the trees to enjoy the forest.

Using deer pathways as a guide, Ferguson began hacking away the underbrush to establish a trail. He supervised the building of wooden bridges to cross the streams, and erected benches and signs. He also planted more trees, such as red woods, and added daffodils.

Ferguson, in addition, uncovered the remains of the old Springfield Copper Mine. The mine produced iron and then copper from 1849 to 1869. It was reopened for a brief period in 1916 and operated as an open-cut mine for hematite-quartz ore.

A handwritten memoir from 1939 states that the shaft was 2800 feet underground (this memoir is part of the Carroll County Historical Society collection). Some local residents also remember when the open hole was used for dumping farm refuse, such as dead animals.

The shaft has been covered and only the outlines of the concrete foundations of the operation remain. Nearby, copper tailings cover part of a slope — a hint, perhaps, that nature cannot always reclaim the waste of man's endeavors.

Ferguson's nature trail is a popular retreat for Fairhaven residents and provides a glimpse of another piece of Sykesville's history.

(64) **Springfield Presbyterian Church.**

Since 1836, Springfield Presbyterian Church has presided on a knoll overlooking the town of Sykesville. The three-story structure of coursed rubble stone covered in stucco is an example of rural Classical architecture. The rectangular-shaped building has a gable-front main facade and is three bays wide. A massive granite stairway leads to the central entrance. A framed doorway and large ten-over-ten sash windows complete the plain, but impressive, front facade.

The church is the oldest one in Sykesville. In August 1835, a group of men met at Brown's Hotel in the village to organize a Presbyterian Church. George Patterson donated land for the site from his Springfield Estate. The cornerstone was laid in May 1836.

A number of influential Marylanders have worshiped in the building including George Patterson and Frank Brown, a past governor of Maryland. In 1837, the church was incorporated as the First Presbyterian Church of Carroll County. Later the name was changed to Springfield Presbyterian.

In the vestibule of the church, windows still have beveled sides with a plain wood sill and no interior frame. The corner stairway features chamfered posts with shaped handrail and square spindles. An original church pew with paneled sides is also in the vestibule. A one-story brick educational wing was added in 1962, and the nave and chancel were remodeled in 1978.

Behind the church is a cemetery in which are graves of the Patterson family and other locally well-known church members.

(65) **Hotel Heights — Frank Brown's Dream.**

It is believed that the flat area at the crest of the hill on Oklahoma Road used to be known as Hotel Heights. However, it should be noted that other sources suggest that the true location for the Heights was actually in the area where the "Dinky Track" crosses Spout Hill Road (no. 55 on Tour 1).

Visitors to Hotel Heights in 1884 could look down on a panorama of steep hills, church spires and train cars curving around the tracks. Frank Brown, in the years before he became Governor, believed the view and the landscape, with its thick chestnut trees, would be the perfect spot for a hotel. A well was dug for it and a roadway prepared, but for unknown reasons the plan was abandoned.

Now several houses are located here.

The Howard County Side of the Patapsco River

The flat land on the Howard County side of the Patapsco has been mostly silent since the flood of 1868 wiped out the busy manufacturing community. Today, very few buildings are left, however, St. Barnabas Episcopal Church, the Hugg-Thomas Wildlife Management Area, and other historic spots tell their own story of early life in Sykesville.

The Warehouse Area

The deceptively peaceful land along the Patapsco River on the Howard County side has attracted only a few businesses since the flood. The Weighing Station and A.H. Renehan & Son were two of those businesses.

The warehouse area in 1929. Photograph courtesy of Orlando V. Wootten.

(66) **The Weighing Station and the Brick and Cinder Warehouse.**

In 1917, the abundant crops of vegetables produced in Howard and south Carroll counties attracted the B.F. Shriver Company. They built a branch factory here to take advantage of the growing market.

The canning company had been founded in Union Mills in 1869 and was one of the pioneers in the processing of vegetables and fruits. "Blue Ridge" and "A No. One Brand" were recognized labels on Shriver products.

At the Sykesville plant, workers packed peas and cream style corn. Older Sykesville residents remember horse-drawn wagons loaded with sweet corn and peas pulling into the clapboard weighing station. The scales were located in the floor. After a wagon was emptied, it was weighed again and the difference was subtracted from the total weight so that the farmer could be paid.

The cannery provided summer work for many local residents until 1931 when the Sykesville plant was closed. The B.F. Shriver Company, however, continued its operations in other parts of Carroll County until the late 1960s.

(67)   **The second home of A.H. Renehan & Son, an apple juice factory.**

Back in 1915, the juice factory that also made apple butter and canned sliced apples for bakeries was located a mile outside of Sykesville on Route 32 in Howard County. The storage bins and a two-story wooden factory building were in a side yard near Renehan's house.

The apple butter was cooked in four huge copper kettles. During World War II, American soldiers in Europe reported getting jars of Renehan's apple butter, as well as sliced apples, as part of their army fare. After the war, Renehan continued to expand, eventually having three shifts of workers (totaling 175 to 200 people) during the peak season of September through January. Apple products under the label "Patapsco Brand" were shipped up and down the East Coast.

After a fire in 1965 destroyed his canning operation on Route 32, Renehan moved his factory to the brick and cinder block storage building that he had purchased from the Shriver Company in 1944. He added a large metal warehouse and made apple juice there until his death in 1986.

Photograph courtesy of William Frederick Church.

(68)   **St. Barnabas Episcopal Church on Forsythe Road.**

The simple, one-story building features sturdy stone work, scalloped verge boards (the wide board edging the gable-end part of the roof), a picturesque belfry, and several handsome stained glass windows. The granite, gable-roofed church is four bays deep and two bays in width.

It is a sad coincidence that the opening of St. Barnabas in 1850 signaled the demise of an older church, Holy Trinity located in Eldersburg. It was built in 1771. The George Warfield family had been active in getting Holy Trinity restored in the 1840s. But, it was a two-hour trip from Sykesville by horse and buggy to attend services there.

Susanna Warfield, especially, wanted another chapel built closer to home. James Sykes, too, was interested in having a more convenient church location. He had brought in a number of English immigrants to work in his mill, many of whom were Episcopalians. Because of the distance to Holy Trinity, he often allowed church services to be held in his hotel.

Between 1845 and 1849, Susanna began her campaign to stimulate interest in the building project. She evidently thought the Holy Trinity Parish would help.

Susanna had participated in a church fair during the summer of 1849, and expected that the money raised would go for the new chapel. She only received one-half of the proceeds and complained that Trinity had not "acted well towards my offspring struggling into existence" (from Susanna Warfield Diaries, MS. 760; Manuscripts Division; Maryland Historical Society Library).

Finally, the cornerstone was laid on the land donated by James Sykes. Several newspapers of the day — The Baltimore American, The Howard Gazette and the Carrolltonean — and several U.S. coins were placed in the cornerstone. But when the church was renovated in 1885, it was discovered that rust and mold had destroyed these items.

Holy Trinity no longer exists, but St. Barnabas still serves its members with regular services. The building was restored in 1981 and has the original stonework, pews and stained glass windows.

In the cemetery east of the church, is a granite railroad stringer with the indentations of the strap rail which was once attached.

The Hugg Mansion. Its burning down on July 22, 1933, precipitated the formation of the Sykesville Volunteer Fire Company. Photograph courtesy of William Frederick Church.

(69) The Hugg-Thomas Wildlife Management Area [across from St. Barnabas with a parking area three-tenths of a mile beyond the Church].

Over 100 years ago, these 276 acres of hardwood forests and rolling hills must have captivated the Hugg brothers — Jacob and John. According to a 1967 article in the Baltimore News American, the brothers came from England in the early 1800s. They became prominent in the shipping industry and built a large home in Baltimore, and one in Sykesville.

Jacob, a sea captain, died in 1870 and left four sons and two daughters. Jacob, Jr. and Maggie were the only ones to survive childhood. Evidently, Jacob, Jr. became a captain like his father, but little else is known about him.

However, an 1884 article in the Howard Gazette stated that Jacob, Jr. was adding a new wing to the house — a wing which had a large three-story bay window. It is said that the Hugg house was built like an old fashioned ship and had a four-story tower. Eventually, the building had 34 rooms. The only other information about Jacob, Jr. comes again from the Howard Gazette in which reference is made to the old sea captain's love of animals. He was described as a man who was "very fond of wild game and fowl and does not allow a feather to be ruffled."

When Maggie Hugg died, she left the Hugg homes and fortune to the family lawyer, William S. Thomas who allowed tenents to farm the land. In 1933, the mansion was destroyed in a fire.

The acreage was deeded as a gift to the State of Maryland by the Maggie V. Hugg Memorial Fund and William S. Thomas of Baltimore in 1936. It was given on the condition that the land be used for a park, or for the Game Division of the Conservation Department.

In an interesting footnote, William S. Thomas (b. 1869, d. 1947) was a bachelor who left the Maryland Historical Society three-quarters of a million dollars. Part of his bequest stipulated that the money be used for a building for the Society and be named "The Thomas and Hugg Memorial." The building was dedicated in 1967.

The Hugg property today is a wildlife management area which has a controlled hunting program. It is opened to the public for hunting by permit only, and, during the season, no more than six hunters per day are allowed. With this type of management, protection and control of wildlife is guaranteed.

Hugg-Thomas is noted for squirrels and doves, as well as deer and some rabbit and pheasant. In addition, rifles are not allowed since Howard County is restricted to shotguns for hunting. The area is very popular for fishing, too, especially bass and blue gill.

Some of the trees on the property are not native to Maryland. It is known that Captain Hugg brought in plants from all over the world. Much of the land that was under cultivation has already been reclaimed by the forests. However, there are about 30 acres of fields and 80 apple trees left, many of them old varieties.

For hunting information call the Maryland Wildlife Administration, Gwynnbrook District Office in Owings Mills, Maryland, (301) 356-9272.

(70) **The Creamery** [private residence].

In the late 1800s and early 1900s, dairy farmers hauled milk to this building. The cream was separated from the milk, and butter was made. Although the building was made into apartments many years ago, older Sykesville residents still refer to the site as "The Creamery."

River Road

River Road, like its namesake, the Patapsco River, meanders and winds through lush, rolling countryside. It used to go behind the Creamery and up a steep hill, and, in the late 1800s and early 1900s, it took six horses to pull a wagon up that incline. When Route 32 and the bridge were rebuilt in 1968, River Road was rerouted in front of the creamery building, and the hill was leveled.

Initially, River Road provided access to several farms bordering the river, including the 300-acre Salopha Estate. Some sections of the road that led from the farms to the nearby railroad tracks no longer exist.   As farming and railroad transportation decreased in importance, single family homes began to spring up in the area. Private access roads became public, and the River Road that begins at Route 32 eventually connected with the Sykesville end at old 32.

As an interesting aside, according to local lore, the big fat rocks in the river were once known as the "Cat Rocks." The origin of that name is now lost to the past, but perhaps they were called such because they were thought to look like sleeping cats, or perhaps because the children used to leap cat-like from one to the next as they crossed the river.

(71) **St. Luke United Methodist Church.**

This is the original site of St. Paul's United Methodist Church before it moved into downtown Sykesville in 1889. The St. Luke congregation had its beginnings in a one room schoolhouse for black children on Schoolhouse Road, but, quite naturally, desired a more appropriate place of worship. St. Paul's donated the vacated land to the congregation, and the Norris family, who have remained one of the pillars of the church for three generations, and others were instrumental in building St. Luke's own official chapel. A cornerstone on the present building, which reads "Oct 9, 1898," testifies to the age of the structure, but restorations over the years have kept it looking new. The congregation is as active now as it was almost one hundred years ago, and, recently, membership has been increasing.

(72) **Gorsuch Switch — once a stop on the Old Main Line of the B & O Railroad.**

The section of River Road that leads to Gorsuch Switch has long been overgrown with scrub and forest and is no longer reachable. In fact, the only evidence left of the rural flag stop is the foundation wall of the bridge. Even Gorsuch Road in Carroll County, which also led to the bridge, no longer exists as a county road.

In 1883, however, Carroll and Howard County farmers must have lobbied hard for a bridge to connect the land which was separated by the Patapsco. Commissioners from both counties met and agreed to build a bridge.

The bridge at Gorsuch Switch was particularly important for the Salopha Farm. The railroad was on the other side of the river in Carroll County, and access to it for the shipping of grain and milk was an economic necessity. Needless to say, the Warfields who owned Salopha provided some of the labor to build the bridge.

Even into the early 1900s, the flag stop was an important destination for area farmers. There was a shelter shed on the eastbound side of the railroad and a siding where fertilizer, lime, hay and grain could be loaded.

Dairy farmers had to have their milk cans at the Gorsuch Switch stop by 7:14 a.m. for the trip to a Baltimore dairy. Doubtlessly to their dismay, the Warfields at nearby Salopha must have known exactly what time the evening train returned the empty milk containers to Gorsuch. The clattering crunch of metal cans striking each other as they were thrown from the train to the platform pierced the country silence for miles around.

The farmers paid ten cents in those days to ride the passenger train to Sykesville. By the time the conductor had collected the money, the train had pulled into the Sykesville station.

It was not uncommon in the early 1900s for the live coals from the engines to start brush fires along the track. Eventually, one such fire destroyed the shelter shed in the 1930s. Hurricane Agnes washed out the bridge in 1972.

(73) **The Eareckson Stone-Log House, 601 River Road   [private residence].**

The central focus of the present structure is a stone one-room slave house that was part of the Tyson property at the Elba Furnace in the 1800s (see pg. 6 in "Tales of Sykesville"). Nearby was a two-story, eight-room log house that may have dated to the 1700s. It was torn down in the mid-1950s, but the logs were used to make a bedroom addition to the stone house.

These logs tell their own tale of the past. The wood is chestnut and has the distinctive cut made only by a broad ax. A closer look at the rough hewn logs reveals both locust pegs, which were used instead of nails, and gun holes.

Other additions to the stone house utilize fieldstone found on the property, beams from buildings that had been burned down in Sykesville, and Georgian pine timbers from old ships.

In front of the stone-log house is a separate guest quarters which was originally a smokehouse. Probably built in the late 1700s, the structure was moved to its present location over an old root cellar in the 1930s. These logs, too, are chestnut and have been cut with a broad ax. An addition to the smokehouse was built with wood from old Sykesville buildings.

(74) **Salopha, 691 River Road.**

Salopha is rich in the early history of both Sykesville and Howard County. The location of the mansion (now on River Road) was near the Patapsco river, the Elba Furnace and the railroad. Sykesville was the nearest town for supplies.

One section of the house, which is two and a half stories, may have been the original log structure built in the 1700s. The south section was built in 1889 and has a center cross gable.

Charles Warfield had purchased Salopha in 1829. According to the Warfield family history, the house and its remaining eighteen acres of land is a remnant of the land owned by a Benjamin Belts in 1723. There is a family myth that an early owner, possibly Benjamin Belts' brother, John, may have negotiated with the Indians to buy the farm, but there is no way to verify the story.

Joshua D. Warfield acquired the property in 1863 from his mother, and built up a prosperous farm of about 340 acres. He also served as a Howard County Commissioner. After Joshua died, Salopha stayed in the Warfield family with Lee Warfield running a dairy operation in the early 1900s.

Lee Warfield sold the farm in 1943. Since then, Salopha has had several owners. From the mid-1950s into the 60s, it was called the Circle X Ranch, and hosted country music stars and rodeos.

Salopha is now owned by Art and Jeri Roemer who are restoring the 18th century mansion. Twice a year, at Christmas and in the spring, they host craft shows. Featured are original works by regional craftspeople and artisans as well as craft demonstrations.

(75) **Howard Lodge.**

A two and one-half story gable-roofed building, Howard Lodge was built in 1750 by Edward Dorsey. Its main feature is its interesting brick work. The exterior walls on the south and east are laid in a Flemish bond pattern, and the west wall in English

bond. The walls are also accented by a brick belt course between the first and second floors.

According to local folklore, the brick was made in England. It has been suggested that at the time bricks were used as ballast for empty ships that were coming to the colonies to pick up tobacco and other goods. While there is no documentary evidence for this practice, it has been alleged that every brick house in Maryland was built this way.

The house is located on what used to be a large tract of land. By the late 1800s, the farm is known to have had about 400 acres producing large crops of wheat, corn and hay. There were also beef and dairy cattle and hogs. Outbuildings included barns, a large blacksmith shop, machinery sheds, a carriage house, and meat and pump houses.

In 1917, Howard Lodge was sold to the B.F. Shriver Company which had just opened a new cannery in Sykesville. Instead of general farming, the Shriver Company grew only canning crops. They also raised beef cattle. The cattle were shipped in by train, and young Sykesville boys would herd the animals to the farm.

Other well-known owners of the property included Francis Scott Key, Jr., son of the patriot. The Keys resided in the house in the late 1850s. One of the later owners of Howard Lodge said that a window pane had been etched with the names "Francis Key and Giles Key." However, this pane of glass and others on the west side of the house were destroyed by hail in June 1917.

Eventually, the farmland was sold as building lots for houses. But the house has been renovated and preserved as one of Howard County's finest buildings.

Map V — Other Historic Spots
in the Sykesville Vicinity

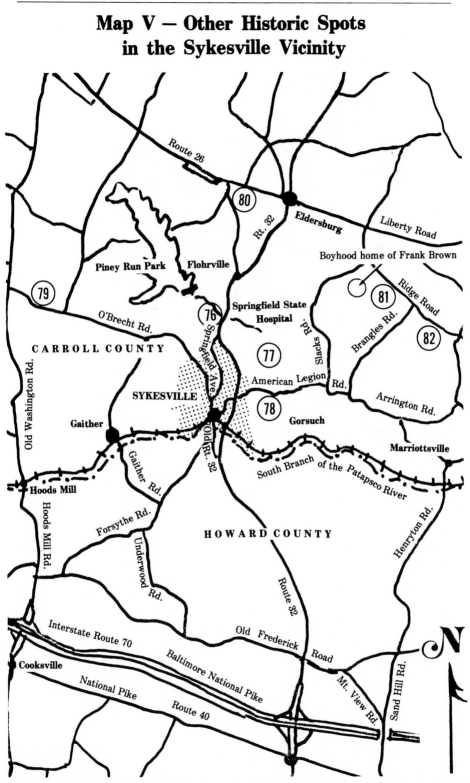

Other Historical Spots in the Sykesville Vicinity

Several places of interest in the Sykesville vicinity are "off the beaten track." However, their history presents another glimpse of what was happening during the town's years of growth. Pictures are included as most of these buildings are not open to the public.

Probably the largest in the United States, this stone burr can still be seen at the Springfield Roller Mills. Photograph taken with the permission of the Buck Family.

⑯ Springfield Roller Mills.

Located on Route 32 near the intersection of Springfield Avenue, the white frame grist mill was built in the early 1800s. It rises three stories, including a large attic area, and has a stone basement.

The mill operated until the mid-1940s, and, in its time, attracted many local farmers who brought in wagon loads of grain. Flour, chicken feed, cornmeal and occasionally graham flour were the main products. "Bonnie Doon" flour was ground here and sent to several East Coast cities.

The stone burr, which is still at the mill, may be the largest one in the United States. It weighs three and one-half tons and measures six feet in diameter.

⑰ Springfield State Hospital.

In 1894, the Maryland Legislature passed a bill creating a new hospital for the more than one thousand mentally ill patients who were then housed in almshouses, jails, and private institutions. After a year's search, a special commission recommended the purchase of Springfield. The site had an abundant water supply, was accessible by train, and was within twenty miles of Baltimore.

Early in 1896, Frank Brown sold 728 acres of the estate, which included the Patterson mansion. By September of that year, twenty-seven patients were living in Buttercup Cottage, a tenant house on the former estate. Through the years additional farm land was bought, and buildings and cottages were constructed.

When the hospital opened in the late 1800s, its goal was to provide permanent lodging and care for patients. It was an "open door" hospital, an innovative concept at the time. None of the patients were locked up and the hospital was a self-sufficient entity.

At times, patients helped in digging potatoes, in farming and in canning vegetables. The hospital managed a large diary farm until the late 1950s and had five

Springfield State Hospital as it appeared in a 1963 copy of the Sykesville Herald.
Photograph courtesy of William Frederick Church.

hundred acres under cultivation until 1968. By that time, there were 3300 patients.

The Sykesville Herald, in the 1960s, described the hospital as a "town larger than the town of Sykesville.... It has its own water system, sewer disposal plant, police force and electric plant. In spite of differences in size, both town and Hospital have prospered through the years and are mutually dependent one upon the other."

By the 1970s, the trend in psychiatric care had moved toward treating and, as soon as possible, discharging patients back into the community. With the advent of more nursing homes, mental health centers and community half-way houses, the patient population decreased. In 1986, there were a little over 900 people being treated.

As a major employer for the area, Springfield Hospital provides an economic base for Sykesville. The institution is often referred to as a family hospital because generations of local families have made their careers there. Despite the decreased number of patients, but due to newer philosophies on the treatment of the mentally ill which require increased patient care, the employee population of the hospital has grown slightly. In 1968, there were 1500 employees and, in 1986, about 1600.

At one time the hospital owned over 1400 acres. Through the years, some of the land has been sold to companies such as Westinghouse. Now the hospital consists of 586 acres and 99 buildings, some of which are not in use. Those first wards built in the 1890s are now empty.

(78) "Raincliffe," or "Chihuahua."

The elegant three-story frame building is an example of the late 19th century grand manor style of architecture. The full height entry porch has massive columns supporting the triangular gable above. A semi-circular window decorates the gable.

The manor has undergone many alterations and a name change since its beginnings in the mid-1800s. George Wethered, a soldier in the Mexican War, had bought and named the property "Chihuahua" in 1856. Just a few years later, he sold it to Charles A. Warfield, whose brother Joshua owned the family home at Salopha.

During the Warfield years, from 1862 to approximately 1917, the farm was the second largest dairy in the region. Only Frank Brown's Springfield was larger.

Warfield enlarged the center of the present building to include 32 rooms, and it became a favorite of the many summer boarders who descended on Sykesville to escape the Baltimore heat. According to newspaper reports of the 1880s, Chihuahua could house 50 guests. The inside was described as being "brilliantly lighted" and as having "soft carpets, rich upholstery and filmy lace curtains."

By the 1930s, the house had been sold, remodeled and reduced to its present size. In 1944, Captain H. C. Jefferson, often referred to as the "dean of the tugboat industry in the United States" bought the house. He renamed the property "Raincliffe," after his grandfather's estate in England.

Captain Jefferson raised cattle for a time at the farm, and at one point he had one of the largest herds of Herfords on the East Coast. He was also active in Sykesville politics, serving as the mayor in the late 1960s and early 70s.

Today, Raincliffe is owned by the State of Maryland. It is being restored through the Department of Natural Resources' private rehabilitation program.

(79) The Mercer House and Farm   [private residence].

The brick for this handsome two-story home was made locally — down in the meadow on the farm. The walls are sixteen inches deep and have always been painted. The original portion of the house was built about 1790. It is two rooms wide and one deep and has an arched cooking fireplace.

The second portion of the house, which is three rooms wide, was built about 1830. The exterior reflects Federal period architecture, especially in the front door which has raised oval panels. The interior is a mixture of late Federal and early Greek Revival, as seen in the fluted pilasters of the mantle.

The dining room has the original floor, chair railing, and built-in dish cupboard. In the center of the ceiling is a handpainted medalion which was a typical decoration of upper middle class homes in the 1830s.

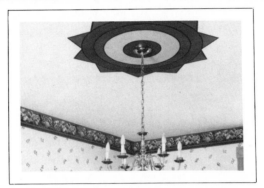

Brightly colored ceiling medalions like this one at the Mercer House were common decorations of upper middle-class homes in the 1830s.

In the early 1900s, the barns on a farm were considered more important than the house. There was a saying back then that the barns, in fact, kept the house. The condition of the barns was an indication as to how productive the land itself was, and a clean and sturdy barn meant a healthy farm.

The 400 acres of the farm have always been cultivated, even in the years before the arrival of the Mercers. By the mid-1800s, the farm had a wood shop and a blacksmith shop, and over them, slave quarters. Also, behind the main house was a smokehouse.

Located four miles from Sykesville, the farm was too far for any kind of town social life. This meant that in the early 1900s the main activities of the children and adults on the farm centered around only the home and the church.

The Mercer family bought the property in 1930, and, like many of their neighbors, they operated a dairy until the early 1980s. One of the most important buildings on the farm was the stanchion barn. Here, cows filed into individual stalls fitted with stanchions or metal pipes that went around their necks. When the stanchions were closed, the cows stayed in place so they could be milked by hand. In 1943, the farm switched to milking machines.

Life on a dairy farm that had 110 cows was not easy. The morning milking began at 4 a.m. There was a second milking in the evening. In the meantime, the cows had to be fed by hand and the barns kept clean. Food for both the animals and people on the farm had to be planted, harvested and stored. In addition to corn and hay, the Mercers planted tomato fields for a nearby canning factory. In the winter, they butchered hogs and hung them in the smokehouse.

The Mercers have now converted to crop farming and raise soy bean, barley and corn.

⑧⓪ Wesley Chapel.

A young carpenter by the name of Forest must have celebrated his birthday while he was building Wesley Chapel in Eldersburg. A board found during the repair of the pulpit in 1920 reads, "John Elder, Contractor. I am 24 years old today, June 24, 1822 — Benjamin Forest."

Now officially recognized by the United States Department of the Interior as an historical landmark, Wesley Chapel is one of the oldest Methodist houses of worship in Carroll County still in use today. But most importantly, it is the only church building that still exists in the same form as it did when it was constructed.

An example of early-nineteenth century vernacular church architecture, its exterior walls are built from rubble masonry construction and simple massing. In line with the simplicity of such rural churches, the interior and exterior details are plain and modest. However, the paneled doors still retain their original hardware, and the pulpit, pulpit rail, and stair balustrade are particularly noteworthy.

In 1939, a number of local Methodist churches were united. Now, the Wesley Chapel is a part of the Wesley-Freedom United Methodist Church.

⑧① The Elias Brown House [private residence].

This two-story, late Georgian style house is one of the few remaining landmarks of the Brown family who were influential landholders in the Eldersburg area. The present 147 acres of farmland surrounding this house are only a fraction of the 2,000 acres acquired and lived on by Abel Brown from 1747 until his death in 1796. He was the great-great grandfather of Maryland's 44th governor, Frank Brown.

Abel's son, Elias Brown, Sr. (b. 1765, d. 1800), inherited a thriving farm and built the stone house in the 1790s. Mexican coins dating back to the 1780s were discovered during the renovation of the house. In addition, he also erected a saw and flour mill which had a cornerstone dated 1798. The mills are no longer in existence.

The most prominent owner, however, was Elias Brown, Jr. (b. 1793, d. 1857), who inherited the house from his father. He was the first Congressman from Carroll County in the U.S. Congress, a member of the Maryland House of Delegates, and a presidential elector for Monroe in 1820 and General Jackson in 1828.

The house itself is typical of the late Georgian style, having a generous central hall flanked by a large room on each side. Halfway up to the second floor, the landing divides. One set of steps leads to a bedroom which features the rope bed that Frank Brown used as a boy (his boyhood home was torn down about 1950 — see map for location). On the other side of the landing is another stairway which leads to two additional bedrooms and a large bath. The downstairs hall and the upstairs have the original, wide, pine flooring.

A two-story kitchen wing that is not as tall as the main house appears to have been built as an addition. The present owners of the house, Mr. and Mrs. Edward Zabel, have uncovered a large, arched cooking fireplace with the original cooking crane. Near the back corner of the fireplace is a small niche which could have been a warming oven or part of a long gone beehive oven.

Beneath the gable, high on the side of the rubble-stone addition, a chiseled block testifies to the age of the building. It reads, "M. B. 1814."

(82) The Moses Brown House.

This is an unusual house which combines an original log structure and an elegant Federal Style addition built approximately 1811 to 1814.

Moses Brown purchased the log house in the 1780s. He was the youngest son of Abel Brown who had deeded portions of his 2,000 acre estate to his descendents. Moses, like his father, was a tobacco grower. By 1813, he had added to his original inheritance and had a total of 937 acres of land.

The log house is a three bay, two-and-a-half story building. It includes three corner fireplaces, two unusual built-in cupboards, and the original boxed stair.

However, Moses's family increased almost as fast as his land holdings, and, by 1812, he had eight children. The rubble-stone addition, comprised of two-stories and an attic, was completed in 1814. The drawing room is particularly striking with its chip-carved Adamesque mantle, the paneled window reveals, and low cupboard flanking the chimney breast. All the woodwork is original.

Moses died in 1817, but the property stayed in his family until 1839. The house is presently being restored.

Index to Sykesville